The
Unexplained
Mysteries of Mind Space
and Time

Open Files

Impossible happenings which have never been explained

Editor: Peter Brookesmith

Orbis Publishing · London

Acknowledgments
Photographs were supplied by Aldus Archive, BBC Hulton
Picture Library, Bildarchiv Preussischer Kulturbestiz,
Canada Press, J-L Charmet, Bruce Coleman, Contemporary
Films, J. Cutten, Adam Hart Davis, Dept of Environment,
Devon and Exeter Instutition Library, E-T Archive,
Elizabeth Picture Library, Mary Evans Picture Library,
Farnham Herald, Flicks, Werner Forman Archive, Fortean
Picture Library, Sonia Halliday, Hertford Museum, Toby
Hogarth, Michael Holford, Keystone Press Agency, Kobal
Collection, F. Millar, R. B. Minton, National Portrait
Gallery, Peter Newark's Western Americana, Nostra, Nova
Scotia Dept of Government Services, Popperfoto, Roger-
Viollet, Robert Runge, Scala, Paul Snelgrove, Society for
Psychical Research, A. F. Stubbs, Suddeutscher-Verlag,
John Topham Picture Library, Harold Wilkins, Zefa.

Consultants to
The Unexplained
Professor A. J. Ellison
Dr J. Allen Hynek
Brian Inglis
Colin Wilson
Editorial Director
Brian Innes
Editor
Peter Brookesmith
Deputy Editor
Lynn Picknett
Executive Editor
Lesley Riley
Sub Editors
Mitzi Bales
Chris Cooper
Jenny Dawson
Hildi Hawkins

Picture Researchers
Anne Horton
Paul Snelgrove
Frances Vargo
Editorial Manager
Clare Byatt
Art Editor
Stephen Westcott
Designer
Richard Burgess
Art Buyer
Jean Hardy
Production Co-ordinator
Nicky Bowden
Volume Editor
Lorrie Mack
Assistants
Ruth Turner
Sarah Reason

© Orbis Publishing Limited, London 1983

First published in the United Kingdom by
Orbis Publishing Limited, London

This edition marketed in the United States of America by
RCA Direct Marketing Inc., 1133 Avenue of the Americas,
New York, New York 10036. U.S.A.

Printed and bound in Italy by Interlitho S.p.A. Milan

Contents

Introduction

MOST OF US enjoy a good mystery: knowing that something is out of joint, a crime has been committed, someone has disappeared, and take pleasure from watching the pieces of the broken jigsaw put slowly and carefully back together again. The classic kind of mystery that works like this is the detective thriller, for not only is the plot tantalisingly unravelled, clue by clue, but in the end justice is seen to be done. And yet the curious thing about mysteries like this is that we go back for more, time and time again. Because it's not really the solution of the plot that we find absorbing: it's the thrill of the chase, the suspense that comes of unsatisfied curiousity. How often do we actually feel a sense of anti-climax when the hero finally catches the villain?

A whole industry has grown up around this realisation that, secretly, we want the mystery to go on for ever. But its products are not to be found under the headings of fiction in the book stores. More often these books masquerade as fact, with titles like *Atlantis rediscovered*, or *More about the Bermuda Triangle*. What the people who write these (often lurid) volumes fail to understand, though, is that it is terribly easy to pull the rug out from underneath such spurious mysteries and tell the world how unlikely they are. And once someone does that, it's very simple to see that the writer in question has not just tried to play a confidence trick on his readers, he's also made it plain that he despised them all along. Not a good way, one would have thought, to remain a popular author.

It's a particularly curious activity to indulge in, too, for the simple reason that there are a vast number of *genuine* unsolved mysteries crying out for serious treatment and a fair hearing – we have gathered some of the most interesting for inclusion in this book.

They range from the eerie story of Joan Norkot who, having been given the chance by being lifted from her grave, pointed out her murderers, dead though she undoubtedly was, by a sign as casual yet as eloquent as a wink. They move through the scarcely less chilling story of the well-to-do Barbados family whose coffins refused to keep still, although they were sealed in the family mausoleum, to the peculiar case of the clergyman who found himself, to all intents and purposes, in contact with the long-dead King Henry VIII. They include straightforward material mysteries such as the unexplained yet enormously elaborate pit built hundreds of feet deep on Oak Island off the coast of Canada, and questions that go to the heart of every human being – as in the strange story of the North African Dogon tribe, who seem to know an extraordinary amount about what goes on in the region of the star Sirius B: so have we, after all, been visited by beings from outer space? Does this mean we are *not* alone in the Universe?

Then we have stories about people whose existence raises more questions than anyone – occasionally including them-selves – can answer. Spring-heeled Jack could certainly have told much about himself had he ever been caught in his escapades, which were considerably less grisly than his later namesake, the Ripper. Some of these bear all the hallmarks of a somewhat over-enthusiastic practical joker, though others were less amusing to the victims. And despite some strong suspicions as to his identity, the prankster has never been conclusively identified.

Kaspar Hauser, on the other hand, acquired a respectable enough name – but absolutely nothing can be said for sure about his actual origins. He simply wandered out of nowhere into a German town – and straight into a controversy about his origins that lasts until today. Was he the illegitimate son of a wealthy noble – someone even of royal blood? An amnesiac? Whatever the answer, and despite the resources of modern scholarship, it looks as if we shall never know the answers – nor the true reason for his death, which was as mysterious as his life.

Then there are animals that have perplexed everyone who has come across their tracks – or, on occasion, had the privilege of seeing them. The most mysterious animal in England is given an outing in these pages – the elusive Surrey puma, still seen from time to time today, but whose heyday was in the 1960s. Quite what an animal better suited to the Rocky Mountains and other inhospitable climes was doing wandering about in populous and leafy southern England is not at all clear. What does seem to have been clearly established, however, is that the animal had not escaped from a zoo, wasn't someone's exotic pet, and had absolutely no intention of being caught. Unlike unexplained or un-known animals of other varieties – bigfeet in particular – the Surrey puma does not seem to have attracted weird pheno-mena of other kinds, such as UFO sightings. It does seem to be a fairly straightforward kind of creature – except that it has a genius for keeping out of the clutches of even the most elaborate hunting parties.

Britain's other odd animal was not thought of at first as an animal at all – at least not by many of those who found its tracks, one cold morning in Devon in the 19th century. As tracks, they weren't especially unusual: what was odd was that they carried on for mile after mile across the count-ryside, deviating occasionally, and unnervingly, to pay a visit to the doors of churches. The rustics promptly said that the Devil had been abroad that night, and doubtless fled home in terror. Learned naturalists tended to believe that a less netherworldly agency had been at work, despite the poss-ibility that Satan in his overweening pride almost certainly would have chosen a snowy night to stalk the earth, if only to ensure maximum publicity. The professors however, were hard put to say just what the creature might have been, so there, more or less, the matter rests.

Possibly the weirdest animals ever reported in the annals

of science were those that disturbed the peace of electrical pioneer Andrew Crosse. While conducting a fairly unremarkable experiment he was suitably astonished to discover that tiny bugs – which he called *acari* – were emerging from the crystalline substance he had concocted. No less a scientist than Michael Faraday was convinced that Crosse had somehow stumbled on a means of creating life – and a fairly complex form of life at that. The possibility that the tiny creatures had already been present in Crosse's equipment was fairly readily dismissed when another experimenter managed to reproduce the results. The world has since steered very clear of this extremely thorny issue, and at the time was reduced to making rude noises about Crosse – as if he had somehow plotted to embarrass and flummox the learned men of the day. In doing so, science actually retreated from the chance to discover, as far as was possible, what had actually occurred in his laboratory that day.

Having opened with the suggestion that when it comes to a mystery we prefer to travel on our journey than to arrive at a solution, it may seem paradoxical that some of the cases in this book do have distinct and definite conclusions. One of the most notorious animals in the history of psychical research, for example, is Gef the talking mongoose. The companion – not to say familiar – of an intelligent teenage girl, Gef caused headlines in the 1930s with the claim that he could speak. That was all very well, but hardly anyone actually clapped eyes on the beast. Few people, for some reason, seem to have been inspired to ask what a mongoose, which likes to live in the tropics and enjoys eating snakes, was doing on a dank island off the coast of England in the first place, but that has not stopped the tale being repeated in sensationalist books and magazine articles for decades. And when one knows the facts as they are detailed here, that is something of a mystery in itself.

Another such tale is the so-called 'haunting' of Lord Dufferin by a spectre who seemed to herald his death. The true story of this oft-repeated legend is rather different, but has rarely seen the light of day. And it seemed only fair to close some of the traditional 'open files', lest it be thought we had missed some really inexplicable cases.

Hence, too, our inclusion of the present, accurate version of the story of the man in the iron mask. This has often been taken to be a mystery as intriguing as the fate of the Dauphin of France at the time of the Revolution, with all kinds of surreal and unlikely characters being suggested as the mysterious masked prisoner. The true story is quite intriguing enough, however, without any embroidery or fantastic additions.

But of all the unexplained feats of story-telling, perhaps the prize goes to the legend of the Indian rope trick. The main features of this astounding display are familiar to almost everyone: the rope that mysteriously stands on end by itself, the boy who climbs up it and whose limbs in due course come tumbling gruesomely from the sky. Of the various theories suggested to account for the rope trick perhaps the most plausible was that some form of mass suggestion was worked by the fakir. But such authentic photographs as did exist of the trick would not bear this out. The rope trick became part of that magic and romantic place, the 'mysterious East', populated by 'inscrutable Orientals' who were capable of working the most powerful spells and performing impossible feats. This is not the place to give away the secret of the rope trick, but it is a mystery whose solution is so stunningly simple that, once more, one is left amazed that anyone was taken in the first time around.

There remains just one more class of 'open file' that we've so far left unmentioned. That is the mysterious place. The moving stones of Racetrack Playa in Death Valley, California, have long attracted attention – and bemusement – for leaving long tracks behind them as they shift about. The only problem is that no-one has ever seen one of these stones move, and though there are a number of plausible theories as to how they do it, no-one is sure that any of them is correct.

Even more peculiar are the events in England's Clapham Wood, where people disappear, strange rites are performed, and UFOs habitually pass by. This is one of those instances of a site of very ancient significance that seems to attract both peculiar phenomena and unusual behaviour, as if the very age of the place itself exerted some power. Or, perhaps, the prehistoric people who first noticed the place were better able than we are to judge that it held some secret, and accordingly made it a sacred place. Whatever the reason, the power of the site seems undiminished even today.

Here then are mystery stories, most of them without heroes or villains – or dramatic endings. Perhaps one day we shall find the answers. But do we really want to?

PETER BROOKESMITH

With a nod or a wink

The old belief that a corpse will react to the presence of its murderer seems to have found horrific expression in the strange case of Joan Norkot. GRAHAM FULLER and IAN KNIGHT investigate the 'impossible' story of the rotting corpse that winked

ONCE DEAD AND BURIED few people have shown signs of life, but those that have, or are rumoured to have been reanimated, have naturally enough inspired the witnesses with awe and fear. In the case of Joan Norkot, who died in 1629, her brief moment of posthumous glory did more; it was enough to point the finger of accusation – almost literally – at her murderers, and subsequently to secure their conviction.

Such was the course of justice in 17th-century England. In those days of widespread superstition it was firmly believed that the body of a murder victim would bleed at the touch of the assassin, and considered binding legal evidence if it did so.

The strange case of Joan Norkot was rediscovered in 1851, when it was one of the legal and historical occurrences selected from the day books of Dr Henry Sampson for inclusion in the July edition of *The Gentleman's Magazine and Historical Review*. In 1851 pragmatism, fact and scientific evidence were the order of the day, as this Victorian journal's prefatory remarks on the case show:

The next extract contains a narrative of a very singular legal case, which comes down to us upon the most unquestionable authority – that of the old Serjeant who, after having been an original member of the Long Parliament of Charles I, lived as father of the bar to congratulate King William on his accession in 1688. . . . It would be difficult to parallel the following relation of superstition and miserable insufficiency of legal proof. . . .

Top: the Long Parliament of 1640, in which John Mainard (above) had sat, living long enough to see William III come to the throne in 1688. Yet his intellect remained as sharp as ever and he was considered an impeccable witness to the bizarre case of Joan Norkot

Left: the resuscitation of Margaret Dickson, a murderer who was hanged in 1728. But Joan Norkot had actually decomposed – how could she have revived?

The 'old Serjeant' in question was one Sir John Mainard, 'a person of great note and judgment in the law', whose version of the Norkot incident was recorded in a manuscript 'fair written with his own hands' and discovered among his papers after his death at the age of 88 in 1690; a copy of it was taken by a Mr Hunt of the Temple, who gave it to Dr Sampson for his records.

Joan Norkot lived in Hertfordshire – it is not known exactly where – with her husband Arthur, her infant son, her sister Agnes and brother-in-law John Okeman, and her mother-in-law Mary Norkot. By all accounts a cheerful, good-looking woman, happily married and a good mother, Joan was well-known to the locals, who expressed surprise and horror when it was revealed that one morning she had been found with her throat cut, apparently the victim of a violent attack, still clutching her child in her arms. Her family claimed that it was suicide.

So had Joan committed suicide? On the night of her death, said Mary Norkot and the Okemans, Joan's husband had been away, visiting friends. They further claimed that there had been 'a deal of trouble' between Arthur and Joan of late, and that on her last

Left: a portrait said to be of Sir Nicholas Hyde, the Lord Chief Justice at Hertford Assizes (below) in 1629 when Joan Norkot's family were tried for her murder. At first it was thought that Joan had committed suicide, but the local people suspected foul play and her body was exhumed. Each member of Joan's family was compelled to touch the grisly remains, which then winked and raised a finger – damning evidence against them in those days. Once the case was brought to court other, more conventional, evidence came to light, and the accused were convicted of Joan's murder and duly hanged – except for her sister-in-law Agnes, who was reprieved because she was pregnant. The motive for the murder remains obscure

evening alive she had been 'in a sour temper, and some despondency'. So maybe, in a fit of despair, she had plunged the knife into her throat. But this was not good enough for Joan's friends and neighbours. In the weeks following the inquest rumour grew to such an extent in the village that it directly challenged the legal verdict. With new evidence coming to light from investigations at the Norkot cottage, it was widely believed that Joan could not have killed herself. Acting on popular opinion,

the jury, whose verdict was not drawn into form by the coroner, desired the coroner that the body, which was buried, might be taken up out of the grave, which the coroner assented to, and thirty days after her death she was taken up, in presence of the jury and a great number of the people.

The touch test

It was at the exhumation, according to the testimony later given in court by the local clergyman, that the test of touch decreed by superstitious custom was made. Mainard takes up the story:

. . . the four defendants present, they were required, each of them, to touch the dead body. Okeman's wife fell on her knees and prayed God to show token of their innocency, or to some such purpose. . . . The appellers did touch the dead body, whereupon the brow of the dead, which was of a livid or carrion colour (that was the verbal expression in the terms of the witness) began to have a dew or gentle sweat [which] ran down in drops on the face, and the brow turned and changed to a lively and fresh colour, and the dead

opened one of her eyes and shut it again, and this opening the eye was done three several times. She likewise thrust out the ring or marriage finger three times and pulled it in again, and the finger dropt blood from it on the grass.

This, in 1629, was irrefutable proof of homicide, and once the furore that necessarily accompanied Joan Norkot's sudden return to the land of the living (and equally abrupt return to eternal sleep) had died down, the jury altered its verdict.

Although it was now declared that Joan Norkot had been 'murdered, by person or persons unknown', the eye of suspicion had come to rest firmly on Arthur, Mary, Agnes and John, and they were subsequently tried at Hertford Assizes – and at first acquitted.

Below: an altar tomb. There are many legends of 'mysterious' rappings coming from such tombs, and of skeletons found bent and twisted inside them. Premature burial was common – comatose or cataleptic people were often thought to be dead and were duly buried, only to die of asphyxiation, thirst or horror. Yet it seems that Joan Norkot was well and truly dead when her body was exhumed, so premature burial can be ruled out as an explanation for her brief reanimation

'The evidence' weighed so heavily against them, however, that presiding Judge Harvy suggested 'that it were better an appeal were brought than so foul a murder should escape unpunished.' Joan Norkot's orphaned son became the plaintiff in the appeal, which was duly lodged against his father, grandmother, aunt and uncle. Said Mainard himself, '. . . because the evidence was so strange I took exact and particular notice of it.' In the trial the events at the graveside were soberly recounted by the local parish minister, described by the chronicler as a 'grave person' but one whose name has not survived.

Not surprisingly, the officiating judge, Chief Justice Nicholas Hyde, doubted the old cleric's evidence. 'Who saw this beside yourself?' he asked the witness. 'I cannot swear that others saw it,' replied the minister, 'but my Lord, I believe the whole company saw it, and if it had been thought a doubt, proof would have been made of it, and many would have attested with me . . . .'

Further, less fantastic evidence was then brought against Mrs Norkot senior and the Okemans, adding to the argument that if no one had gone into the cottage between the time when Joan retired for the night and when she was found dead, then they must be her murderers. Joan had been found lying in her bed with the bedclothes undisturbed, and her child with her – indicating that suicide had not taken place in the bed, in fact not at all. Her throat was cut from ear to ear and her neck broken, and if she first cut her throat, she could not break her neck while lying in the bed, or vice versa.

Murder most foul

Clearly the dead body had been moved and there had been a half-hearted attempt to conceal the evidence. Moreover, the bloody knife had been firmly embedded in the floor some distance from the bed, point towards the bed, haft towards the door. However violent her death throes, there is no way that Joan Norkot – had she actually taken her own life – could have thrown the blade into that position. Lastly, there was the bloody print of a left hand on top of Joan's own left hand, an item of evidence that Chief Justice Hyde questioned but eventually accepted.

The four prisoners were then brought forward but had no defence to offer. Arthur Norkot's alibi collapsed when it was revealed that he had not visited the friends he had claimed to be staying with for several years. The jury retired and when it returned found Norkot, his mother and Agnes guilty of murder. Okeman was acquitted. The three guilty persons each cried out, 'I did not do it! I did not do it!' but, nevertheless, judgement was passed. Norkot and his mother were sentenced to death and duly hanged, but Agnes Norkot was reprieved when it was discovered she was pregnant.

In his reconstruction and discussion of the case in *Unsolved mysteries* (1952), Valentine Dyall suggests a possible – though speculative – reason for the murder:

> The motive for the crime remained obscure, though it was generally supposed that Arthur Norkot had believed his wife unfaithful. The other two women of the family, known to be jealous of Joan's good looks and position as mistress of the house, probably made willing accomplices – while John Okeman, a simple fellow, was bullied into silence.

But there is no logical explanation for the incredible scene that took place when Joan was disinterred. We can toy with the notion of premature burial, but there can be no doubt that Joan Norkot was well and truly deceased when she was laid to rest. Perhaps exposure to the elements had an immediate chemical effect on her decaying flesh, explaining the 'lively and fresh colour' of her brow, but how did Joan's eye wink, and her finger move and yield fresh blood?

Maybe it was just that Joan Norkot, in the course of divine retribution, awoke fleetingly from death to ensure that justice was done.

Memories of a distant star?

The Dogon people of West Africa have a detailed knowledge of the Universe that is astonishingly accurate. But, asks FRANCIS HITCHING, how did they obtain this knowledge? Was it, as the Dogon claim, passed on by ancient astronauts?

LIKE MANY AFRICAN TRIBES, the Dogon people of the Republic of Mali have a shadowed past. They settled on the Bandiagara Plateau, where they now live, some time between the 13th and 16th centuries. It is about 300 miles south of Timbuktu, for most of the year a desolate, arid, rocky terrain of cliffs and gorges dotted with small villages built from mud and straw.

Although most anthropologists would class them as 'primitive', the 2 million people who make up the Dogon and surrounding tribes would not agree with this epithet. Nor do they deserve it, except in the sense that their way of life has changed little over the centuries. Indifferent though they are to

Below: a Dogon settlement at the foot of the Bandiagara cliffs. The Dogon are a primitive people, yet they have a profound belief that they were originally taught and 'civilised' by beings from outer space – from the star system Sirius

Right: Sirius lies in the constellation Canis Major, near the foot of Orion. It can be readily identified as it sits in a line with the three bright stars of Orion's belt

Western technology, their philosophy and religion is both rich and complex. Outsiders who have lived with them, and learned to accept the simplicity of their lives, speak of them as a happy, contented, fulfilled people whose attitude to the essential values of life dates back millennia.

Unremarkable enough so far – but the Dogon make one astounding claim. They believe, with absolute certainty, that they were originally taught and 'civilised' by creatures from outer space: specifically, from the star system Sirius, 8.7 light years away.

And they back up this claim with what seems to be extraordinarily detailed knowledge of astronomy for such a 'primitive' and isolated tribe. Notably, they know that Sirius, the brightest star in the sky, has a companion star, invisible to the naked eye, which is small, dense, and extremely heavy. This is perfectly accurate. But its existence was not even suspected by Western astronomers until the middle of the 19th century; it was not described in detail until the 1920s, and not photographed (so dim is this star, called Sirius B) until 1970.

Yet this curious astronomical fact forms the central tenet of Dogon mythology. It is enshrined in their most secret rituals, portrayed in sand drawings, built into their sacred architecture, and can be seen in carvings, and patterns woven into their blankets, whose designs almost certainly date back hundreds, if not thousands, of years.

It has been held as the most persuasive evidence yet that Earth had, in its fairly recent past, an interplanetary connection – a close encounter of the educational kind. The extent of Dogon knowledge has also been looked at extremely sceptically, to establish whether all that they say is true, and if true, whether their information may not have

Above left: Sirius, the brightest star in the sky, and its white dwarf companion Sirius B. This tiny star is so dim that it was not photographed until 1970 – yet the Dogon have always made sand drawings portraying Sirius accompanied by another star

Above: Marcel Griaule and Germaine Dieterlen (top), the two French anthropologists who lived with the Dogon tribe for over 20 years, and to whose careful study we owe much of our knowledge of Dogon mythology

Right: cave paintings depicting the myths of the Dogon people

come from an Earthbound source – a passing missionary, say.

So first, how did we in the West come to know of the Dogon beliefs? There is just one basic source, which fortunately is a very thorough one. In 1931 two of France's most respected anthropologists, Marcel Griaule and Germaine Dieterlen, decided to make the Dogon the subject of extended study. For the next 21 years they lived almost constantly with the tribe. In 1946 Griaule was invited by the Dogon priests to share their innermost sacred secrets. He attended their rituals and their ceremonies, and learned, so far as it was possible for any Westerner to do so, the enormously complex symbolism that stemmed from their central belief in the amphibious creatures, which they called Nommo, that had come from outer space to civilise the world. Griaule himself came to be revered by the Dogon as much as their priests. At his funeral in Mali in 1956, a quarter of a million tribesmen gathered to pay him homage.

The findings of the two anthropologists were published first in 1950, in a cautious and scholarly paper entitled 'A Sudanese Sirius System' in the *Journal de la Société des Africainistes*. After Griaule's death, Germaine Dieterlen remained in Paris, where she was appointed Secretary General of the Société des Africainistes at the Musée de

l'Homme. She wrote up their joint studies in a massive volume entitled *Le renard pâle*, the first of a planned series, published in 1965 by the French national Institute of Ethnology.

The two works make it overwhelmingly clear that the Dogon belief system is indeed based on a surprisingly accurate knowledge of astronomy, mingled with a form of astrology. Lying at the heart of it is Sirius, and the various stars and planets that they believe to orbit around it. They say that its main companion star, which they call *po tolo*, is made of matter heavier than anything on Earth, and moves in a 50-year elliptical orbit.

All these things are true. Western astronomers first deduced that something curious was happening around Sirius about 150 years ago. They noted certain irregularities in its motion which they could explain only by postulating the existence of another star close to it, which was disturbing Sirius's movements through the force of gravity. In 1862 the American astronomer Alvan Graham Clark actually spotted the star when testing a new telescope, and he called it Sirius B.

However, it took another half-century from the first observation of Sirius's peculiarities until a mathematical and physical explanation could be found for why such a small object was exerting such massive force. Sir Arthur Eddington, in the 1920s, formulated the theory of certain stars being 'white dwarfs' – stars near the end of their life that have collapsed in on themselves and become superdense.

The description fitted the Dogon version precisely. But how could they have learned about it in the three years between Eddington's announcement of the theory in a popular book in 1928, and the arrival of Griaule and Dieterlen in 1931? The two anthropologists were baffled: 'The problem of knowing how, with no instruments at their disposal, men could know of the movements and certain characteristics of virtually invisible stars has not been settled.'

At this point another researcher entered the scene: Robert Temple, an American scholar of Sanskrit and Oriental Studies living in Europe, who became deeply fascinated by the two questions raised by the Dogon enigma.

First, was the evidence of the Dogon understanding of astronomy to be believed? And second, if the answer to the first question was positive, how could they conceivably have come by this knowledge?

A careful reading of the source material, and discussions with Germaine Dieterlen in Paris, convinced him after a time that the Dogon were indeed the possessors of an ancient wisdom that concerned not just Sirius B, but the solar system in general. They said the Moon was 'dry and dead like dry dead blood'. Their drawing of the planet Saturn had a ring round it (two other exceptional cases of primitive tribes privy to this information are known). They knew that planets revolved round the sun, and recorded the movements of Venus in their sacred architecture. They knew of the four 'major moons' of Jupiter first seen by Galileo (there are now known to be at least 14). They knew correctly that the Earth spins on its axis. They believed there was an infinite number of stars, and that there was a spiral force involved in the Milky Way, to which Earth was connected.

Since much of this came down in myth and symbolism, in which objects on Earth were said to represent what went on in the skies, and in which a concept of 'twinning' made many of the calculations obscure, it could not be said that the evidence was totally unambiguous. But with Sirius B in particular the central facts seemed unarguable. The Dogon deliberately chose the smallest yet most significant object they could find – a grain of their essential food crop – to symbolise Sirius B: *po tolo* means literally a star made of *fonio* seed. They stretched their imaginations to describe how massively heavy its mineral content was: 'All earthly beings combined cannot lift it.'

Temple found the sand drawings particularly compelling. The egg-shaped ellipse might perhaps be explained away as representing the 'egg of life', or some such symbolic

Below: grain stores in a Dogon settlement. The doors to the granaries (right) are decorated with painted figures depicting the tribe's heavenly ancestors

meaning. But the Dogon were insistent that it meant an orbit – a fact discovered by the great astronomer Johannes Kepler in the 16th century, but certainly not known to untutored African tribes. And they also put the position of Sirius within the orbit exactly where it ought to be rather than where someone might naturally guess it: that is, at a focal point near the edge of the ellipse, rather than in the centre.

So how did the Dogon come to have this unearthly knowledge? Here, so far as the priests were concerned, there was no ambiguity whatsoever in the answer: they believe profoundly that amphibious creatures from a planet within the Sirius system landed on Earth in distant times and passed on the information to the initiates, who in turn handed it down over the centuries. They call the creatures Nommos, and worship them as 'the monitor of the universe, the father of mankind, guardian of its spiritual principles, dispenser of rain and master of the water'.

Temple found that the Dogon drew sand diagrams to portray the spinning, whirling descent of a Nommo 'ark', which he takes to mean a spaceship:

The descriptions of the landing of the ark are extremely precise. The ark is said to have landed on the earth to the north-east of the Dogon country, which is where the Dogon claim to have come from originally.

The Dogon describe the sound of the landing of the ark. They say the 'word' of Nommo was cast down by him in the four directions as he descended, and it sounded like the echoing of the four large stone blocks being struck with stones by the children, according to special rhythms, in a very

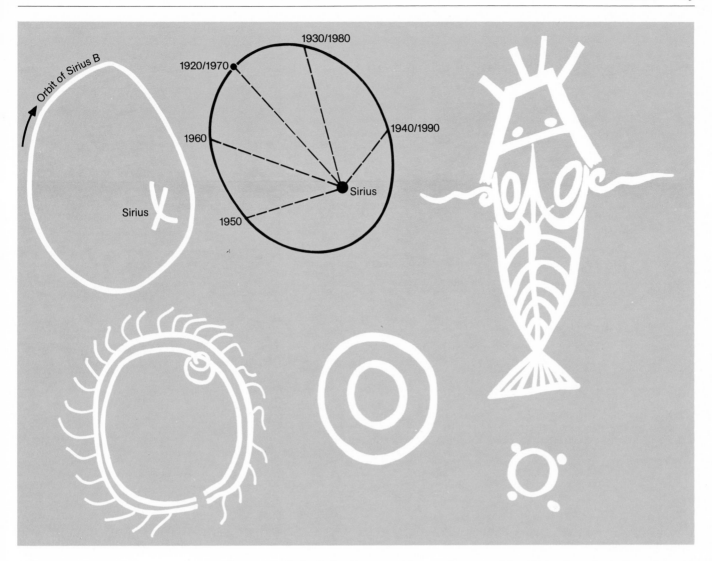

Tribal drawings of the Nommo (top right), the amphibious creatures said to have given the Dogon information about the solar system, and of the descent of the ark (above), the 'spaceship' in which the Nommo travelled. The Dogon's knowledge of astronomy is illustrated in their drawings: their portrayal of the orbit of Sirius B around Sirius (top left) is remarkably similar to a modern astronomical diagram (top centre); they show Saturn with its ring (above centre), and depict the four 'major moons' of Jupiter discovered by Galileo (above right)

small cave near Lake Debo. Presumably a thunderous vibrating sound is what the Dogon are trying to convey. One can imagine standing in the cave and holding one's ears at the noise. The descent of the ark must have sounded like a jet runway at close range.

Other descriptions that the Dogon priests used to refer to the landing of the 'ark' tell how it came down on dry land and 'displaced a pile of dust raised by the whirlwind it caused. The violence of the impact roughened the ground . . . it skidded.'

Robert Temple's conclusions, first published in 1976 in his book *The Sirius mystery*, are at once highly provocative and extensively researched. As such, his findings have been used as ammunition both by those who believe in extra-terrestrial visitations in Earth's formative past, and by those (including the majority of scientists and historians) who believe the idea is bunkum.

Erich von Däniken, for instance, whose best-selling books on the subject have now been shown to be based, in the main, on distorted evidence, has welcomed the Dogon beliefs, calling them 'conclusive proof . . . of ancient astronauts'. Against him range a number of science writers – among them Carl

Sagan and Ian Ridpath – who believe the case is by no means proved, and that Temple has read too much into Dogon mythology.

Robert Temple himself, 10 years after first becoming interested in the subject, found nothing to retract from the answer he gave to his publisher, who expressed his central doubt about the manuscript thus: 'Mr Temple, do you believe it? Do you believe it *yourself*?'

Temple answered: 'Yes, I do. I have become convinced by my own research. In the beginning I was just investigating. I was sceptical. I was looking for hoaxes, thinking it couldn't be true. But then I began to discover more and more pieces which fit. And the answer is *yes, I believe it*.'

The crucial question is whether the Dogon's knowledge could have been obtained in any ordinary, mundane way. Was this apparently arcane, obscure and detailed astronomical information given to them by the Nommo – or was it simply obtained from Westerners and rapidly absorbed into their mythology?

The amphibians from outer space

Did ancient astronauts civilise the Earth? And could they have come from a third star in the Sirius system, a star not yet discovered by Western astronomers?

WEST AFRICA'S DOGON TRIBE, some 2 million people, have a complex mythology built around the belief that, at some time in the distant past, amphibian beings called Nommo visited Earth with the purpose of civilising it. The Dogon revere the Nommo, who, they say, come from the star system Sirius, the brightest in the sky. They make sand drawings to show that Sirius has two invisible companion stars. One is small and extremely dense, 'heavier than all the material on Earth'. The other is said to be four times lighter in weight, and to have a nearly circular orbit. It is from a planet attached to this latter star that the Nommo are believed by the Dogon to have descended.

Stories of extra-terrestrial visitations are difficult to incorporate within modern science, and it is not surprising that the Dogon claims have been strongly and sceptically scrutinised. Writers who seek to give a plausible and terrestrial explanation of the Dogon's uncanny knowledge have pointed out that there have been French schools incorporating geography and natural history in their curricula in the area since 1907; that there has been a Moslem university in nearby Timbuktu since the 16th century; and even that members of the Dogon are said to have fought for the French in the trenches during the First World War. Robert Temple, however, thinks such explanations are facile:

> The two French anthropologists [Marcel Griaule and Germaine Dieterlen] started their work in 1931, and they are positive that the Dogon knew details about Sirius B when they arrived. . . . Eddington revealed the superdensity of Sirius B around 1926. . . . So there is a narrow period . . . when one has to imagine some group of amateur Western astronomers rushing out to . . . Mali and implanting this knowledge in the presumably pliant minds of the Dogon.

Temple is supported by Germaine Dieterlen, who lived with the Dogon for more than three decades. Any suggestion that the astronomical knowledge was of recent origin was, she said, absurd.

On balance it does not seem as if the

Left: Oannes, the fish-bodied deity of Babylon. According to Babylonian tradition, Oannes was the leader of the Annedoti, a group of amphibious beings who founded civilisation

Dogon information came from modern Western sources – at least according to the researchers who have lived in and studied the area. But the evidence is by no means unambiguous, and there are only two ways of reaching a sound judgement about the extraordinary Dogon beliefs: first, to see if there is any supportive evidence in other legends from other places; and second, to see if there is any claim made by the Dogon that can be scientifically tested.

We are in the fortunate position of being able to make both approaches. The Dogon description of the Nommo is quite clear – they were amphibians, and they had a civilising, life-giving role. And their description of two invisible stars orbiting Sirius is intensely interesting, for although one (a so-called white dwarf) has already been discovered by Western astronomers, the other has not yet been. If the Dogon turned out to be correct in this, it would be powerful confirmation of the rest of their mythology.

In antiquity, the Dogon were almost certainly neighbours of the Egyptians, living in North Africa on the shores of the Mediterranean. So it is the classical mythologies – Egyptian, Mesopotamian and Greek – that must be examined to see if there are parallel legends speaking of Sirius as something special in the sky, and of being the home of amphibian visitors from outer space.

It is a difficult task even for classical scholars. In his book *The Sirius mystery*, Robert Temple points out that the Dogon knowledge, until unearthed by two trusted French anthropologists, was sacred and secret to the priesthood. Similarly with classical legends.

Secret doctrines are not scribbled down too frequently and left for posterity. The most secret doctrine of the

Above: the two medallions worn by this Dogon woman are said to signify the 'twinning' concept of Dogon mythology – the notion that each element of nature is one of a pair of opposites

Dogon was only revealed with great reluctance after many, many years, and following upon a conference by the initiates. The Egyptians were no fools, and we can hardly expect them to have left papyri or texts specifically revealing in so many words what they were not supposed to reveal. We can only try to piece together clues.

In Temple's view, the clues 'turn into a veritable avalanche'. But about the star system Sirius itself the myths tell us disappointingly little. Peter James, a classical historian at London University, points out that it is hardly surprising that the ancients regarded Sirius as an important star and attached to it a number of mythological motifs. Sirius was not only the brightest star in the sky, but for many centuries its heliacal rising coincided with the inundation of the Nile, giving it a special calendrical importance. 'None of the myths as they stand obviously describe the kind of knowledge about Sirius' invisible astronomy such as the Dogon appear to possess – nothing suggests extraordinary knowledge of Sirius B.'

As an example of how far one has to stretch interpretation of myths in order to read into them an occult knowledge of Sirius's companion star, Peter James quotes the Isis/Osiris relationship as the best of Robert Temple's 'clues'. It is, to say the least, obscure:

Isis, the goddess of Sirius, had a husband called Osiris, who was considered dark, or black. One of his aspects was Anubis, a Jackal-headed god. There is not much to go on here, but it at least suggests the possibility that the Egyptians knew about an invisible companion to Sirius A.

However, the parallels between Greek and

Left: in ancient Egyptian mythology, the dog god Anubis is often identified with Osiris, companion of the goddess Isis. Historian Robert Temple considers that as Isis herself was identified with Sirius, it is reasonable to suppose that her companion was identified with the companion of Sirius – suggesting that the ancient Egyptians knew of the existence of Sirius B

Dogon legends about civilising amphibian creatures are much more promising. Fish-bodied aliens abound in Greek mythology, notably in the island of Rhodes, with its culture-bearing inhabitants the Telchines.

Diodorus Siculus, the Greek historian, wrote of them that they were 'the discoverers of certain arts and introduced other things which are useful for the life of mankind.' Other texts speak of them being 'submarine magic spirits' and 'demons of the depths of the sea'; they 'had dog's heads and flippers for hands'.

From Berossus, a Babylonian priest, there is a very similar description of creatures called Annedoti ('Repulsive Ones'), fish-men who introduced civilisation. The first and most famous was called Oannes or Oe, who was thought to have come from a great egg, and who instructed the Babylonians 'in

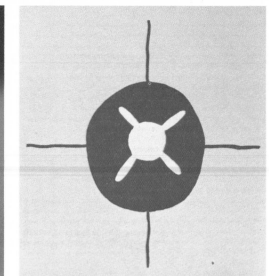

Above right: a Dogon drawing portraying the heliacal rising of Sirius. The Dogon claim their knowledge of such astronomical events came from the Nommo; but the ancient Egyptians knew of the rising of the star and based their calendar on it – could they have given the information to the Dogon?

Above: an altar object, depicting seven Nommo figures, from a Dogon shrine

Left: the hounds of Actaeon. According to Greek legend these were the survivors of the Telchines, amphibian, life-giving gods of Rhodes

every thing which could tend to soften manners and humanize mankind'.

Peter James's cautious conclusion is 'there does seem to be a substratum of Greek myth that connects fish-deities with the introduction of civilisation and the oracles, that has parallels in the traditions of the Dogon and the Babylonians.'

None of this, of course, is as conclusive as would be the discovery of a third star in the Sirius system, as predicted by the Dogon. For the time being, once again the signs are not promising, but within the bounds of possibility. Indeed, the matter has been the subject of considerable astronomical debate.

In the 1920s, a number of astronomers repeatedly said they had observed a third star, and named it Sirius C. It was perceived as being red, so it could be what is known as a red dwarf, which is much less dense than a white dwarf. This would be consistent with the Dogon description of the third star being four times lighter (in weight) than Sirius B.

Subsequently, it has not been possible to observe the star. Also, perturbations in the

movement of Sirius A, which were thought to be linked to a possible third star, have now been shown to be unconnected. The astronomer who provided this 'disproof', Irving W. Lindenblad at the US Naval Observatory in Washington, DC, thinks the existence of a third star highly unlikely: 'The possibility of a *very distant* third body cannot be ruled out theoretically as being physically impossible but there is absolutely no evidence for such a body.' Two astronomers at London University, writing in the technical journal *Astrophysics and space science*, were slightly more optimistic: they had produced on a computer near-circular orbits (as described by the Dogon) lasting from 275 to 425 years for a third star that would be consistent with the motion of Sirius A.

So where does this argument and counter-argument leave us? Are the Dogon traditions good evidence of extra-terrestrial visitors?

It is fair to conclude that, somehow or another, they are privy to astronomical information, which by right they should not be. This is the considered opinion of Germaine Dieterlen, and it seems preferable to accept her first-hand judgement than that of her (and Temple's) critics who re-interpret the myths at second hand.

But where did the knowledge derive? Is the misty link between the amphibians of Greek and Babylonian legend and the Dogon Nommo enough to make us sure that Earth has been visited in the past? It is so unlikely a possibility that before embracing it we might also consider other unlikely explanations: that the priesthoods of classical times formed their knowledge of the Universe through extra-sensory perception, using secret oracular methods that we have long forgotten, but that percolated into the mythology of the Dogon priesthood. Perhaps, against all the astronomical odds, the third star in the Sirius system, a supposed red dwarf, flared so violently that it could be seen and its orbit calculated. It is, you might say, a balance of improbabilities.

From a remote hilltop on the Isle of Man there came, in the 1930s, news of an amazing talking animal – a mongoose that was often heard but seldom seen. MELVIN HARRIS investigates the story of 'Gef' and the family he haunted

THE AFFAIR of the talking mongoose caused a great deal of excitement in the early 1930s. Initially called the 'talking weasel', this amazing creature lived in a remote place on the Isle of Man and, so the newspaper accounts said, did not just repeat words like a parrot. It used words with an understanding of their meaning. Indeed, according to the family with whom the creature lived, it gave direct answers to questions and made spontaneous comments – some of them quite witty and knowledgeable.

The animal haunted a place called Doarlish Cashen, an isolated farmstead perched over 700 feet (215 metres) up on the west coast of the island. It was a cheerless terrain without trees or shrubs. Even the nearest neighbours were out of view, over a mile (1.6 kilometres) away. Ordinarily there would be little to attract anyone to Doarlish Cashen. But, in September 1931, the rumours of the talking weasel sent the journalists scrambling up the forbidding hill to meet the Irving family who lived at the farm.

A rare picture of Gef, the talking mongoose – centre of a media sensation in the early 1930s. Usually Gef would not show himself even to the family with whom he lived – or whom he haunted – on the Isle of Man. But, so the family said, he allowed this photograph to be taken by Voirrey Irving, the daughter of the house. The wonderful talking animal, often witty and as often insulting, managed to elude all his many investigators

The head of the family was James Irving, a retired commercial traveller approaching 60. An intelligent man with mild, benign features, he was known as an engaging talker and raconteur. He seemed to keep his cheerfulness and good humour despite the fact that his farmstead production had steadily declined, reducing his income to a mere 15 shillings a week.

His wife Margaret was a few years younger than he. She was said to be tallish with a 'dignified bearing, upright and square of carriage'. Her grey hair rose primly above her forehead '. . . to frame her most compelling feature – two magnetic eyes that haunt the visitor with their almost uncanny power'. It was all too easy to draw the conclusion that Margaret Irving was the dominant personality in the household.

The Irvings' daughter Voirrey was 13 but old for her years. She seemed a reserved and undemonstrative child, hardly a scholar but obviously intelligent. And she took an intelligent and eager interest in anything to do with animals, reading any article or book she could get that dealt with them. By contrast, she was also fascinated by mechanical devices such as motor cars, aeroplanes and cameras.

Voirrey's knowledge of animals was not just theoretical but also practical. She was

The mongoose that talked

fully experienced in handling sheep and goats. And she had devised a successful way to catch rabbits. She would roam the hills with her sheepdog Mona until a rabbit was sighted. While Mona 'pointed' the prey and put it in a frozen mesmerised state, Voirrey would slowly creep up behind and kill the rabbit with a sharp blow to the head. The significance of her skills in this regard came out later.

Of the many newspaper reporters who met the Irvings, the luckiest came from the Manchester *Daily Dispatch*, for he was the only one to hear the talking weasel. He wrote of his successful mission:

> The mysterious 'man-weasel' . . . has spoken to me today. Investigation of the most remarkable animal story that has ever been given publicity . . . leaves me in a state of considerable perplexity. Had I heard a weasel speak? I do not know, but I do know that I've heard today a voice which I should never have imagined could issue from a human throat.

He left the house puzzled and impressed but fully convinced that the Irvings were honest and responsible – unlikely to be the initiators

Right: the Irving family in their ill-lit home, known as Doarlish Cashen. From the left are Voirrey, her mother Margaret and her father Jim

Below: Voirrey and her dog Mona. Some investigators hinted that Gef might be the creation of this lonely and intelligent girl, but this was not proved conclusively

of an elaborate and sustained practical joke.

His next report, however, was more guarded:

> Does the solution of the mystery of the 'man-weasel' of Doarlish Cashen lie in the dual personality of the 13-year-old girl, Voirrey Irving? That is the question that leaps to my mind after hearing the piercing and uncanny voice attributed to the elusive little yellow beast with a weasel's body. . . . Yesterday I heard several spoken sentences. . . . The conversation was between the 'weasel-voice' and Mrs Irving, who was unseen to me in another room, while the girl sat motionless in a chair at the table. I could see her reflection, although not very clearly, in a mirror on the other side of the room. She had her fingers to her lips. . . . The lips did not move, so far as I could see, but they were partly hidden by her fingers. When I edged my way into the room the voice ceased. The little girl continued to sit motionless, without taking any notice of us. She was sucking a piece of string, I now saw.

Remarkably, none of the eager visitors ever caught sight of the talking animal. They all had to rely on Jim Irving's description to picture it. He judged it to be about the size of 'a three-parts grown rat, without the tail' and thin enough to pass through a $1\frac{1}{2}$-inch (4-centimetre) diameter hole. Its body was yellow like a ferret's, its long bushy tail was tinged with brown, and its face was shaped somewhat like a hedgehog's but with a flattened, pig-like snout. This description was based on the pooled information of the three

Irvings, for each of them claimed to have seen the animal on separate occasions.

According to Jim Irving, their tiny lodger had first made itself known by barking, growling and spitting – all purely animal sounds. Irving took the sudden notion to try to teach the creature other kinds of noises. So he began to imitate animal and bird sounds and to name each creature as he made its sound. Within days, he claimed, the weasel would repeat the sounds as soon as the relevant animal or bird name was called out. The most astounding part of his experiment soon followed. 'My daughter then tried it with nursery rhymes, and no trouble was experienced in having them repeated.'

From then on there was no stopping the wily weasel. By February 1932 it was freely demonstrating its remarkable cleverness to the Irvings. Jim Irving wrote:

It announces its presence by calling either myself or my wife by our Christian names. . . . It apparently can see in the dark and described the movements of my hand. Its hearing powers are phenomenal. It is no use whispering: it detects the whisper 15 to 20 feet [4.5 to 6 metres] away, tells you that you are whispering, and repeats exactly what one has said.

When the ghost hunter Harry Price learned of the talking weasel, he acted swiftly by asking a colleague to visit the Irvings and file a report. Price called this investigator 'Captain Macdonald' to protect him from any unwanted publicity. Macdonald obliged and turned up at the farmhouse on the evening of 26 February 1932. There he sat around for almost five hours – and heard and saw nothing. But as he left the place, he heard a shrill scream from inside the house – 'Go away. Who is that man?' The words were quite clear at first, then they tailed away into unintelligible squeals. When Macdonald hurried back into the house, the voice ceased. So he arranged to return early the next day.

The next day's vigil started with the Captain being shown some water trickling from a hole in the wall. He was solemnly assured that this was 'the animal performing its natural functions'. The vigil proved more fruitful later. In the evening, Voirrey and her mother went into the bedroom above the living room and within minutes a shrill voice started talking to Margaret Irving. This went on for a quarter of an hour. Then Macdonald appealed to the animal to show itself. 'I believe in you!' he shouted, hoping to charm the evasive weasel. But the squealed reply was final. 'No, I don't mean to stay long as I don't like you!' Macdonald then tried to creep up the stairs but slipped, making a deafening clatter. With that the creature screamed, 'He's coming!' So ended Macdonald's hoped-for ambush.

Ten days later, Charles Northwood –

Doarlish Cashen, high on a cheerless hilltop with the nearest neighbour more than a mile (1.6 kilometres) away. The ramshackle house gave Gef plenty of scope for playing hide and seek

again, not his real name – turned up at Doarlish Cashen. An old friend of Jim Irving, he came out of concern for the Irvings, and later he sent a favourable report to Price. By now, the family had christened the talking animal 'Gef' and had discovered that he was an Indian mongoose born in Delhi on 7 June 1852. These details 'came from Gef himself'.

Once Northwood had settled in, Irving called out, 'Come on Gef, Mr Northwood's here. You promised to speak you know!' But not a squeak was heard – until Voirrey went into the kitchen to prepare lunch. Then in a mild voice Gef said, 'Go away Voirrey, go away.' Two minutes later Gef began to speak again. Then, when Irving asked him to bark,

Right: Jim Irving points to Gef's fingers appearing through the slats on the bedroom wall. All the pictures of the talking mongoose were uniformly poor and indistinct, leaving as much to the imagination as to the eye

Below: the wooden box-like structure known as 'Gef's Sanctum', located in Voirrey's room. On top is a chair that, according to the Irvings, the mongoose pushed around for exercise

he promptly did so. But he refused to sing his favourite song *Carolina moon*, even though the gramophone record was played to inspire him. Later still, Gef shouted, 'Charlie, Charlie, Chuck, Chuck . . . Charlie my old sport! . . . Clear to the Devil if you don't believe!'

Gef's mood changed when he heard that Northwood's son, Arthur, was due to arrive at the Irving farm. He grew threatening. 'Tell Arthur not to come. He doesn't believe. I won't speak if he does come. I'll blow his brains out with a thruppenny cartridge!'

Then he softened a little and returned to domestic small talk. 'Have you ordered the rooster, James, from Simon Hunter? Mind you do so. Have you posted that letter?' But a short while later his vicious side took over again. As Northwood put it:

. . . from behind the boards in the sitting room, possibly some 25 to 30 feet [8 to 9 metres] away, I heard a very loud voice penetrating, and with some malice in it: 'You don't believe. You are a doubter,' etc. This was very startling, and for the first time put a bit of a shiver through me. Equal to a couple of irascible women's voices put together! I said: 'I do believe.' I had to shout this.

Then came the probing query, 'Charlie. . .is Arthur coming?' followed by a screech and a loud thump.

By this time Northwood had to leave, which meant the end of the encounter. But on his way down the hill he heard some screeches behind him and each of these was identified by Irving as having been made by Gef.

Northwood made a second visit a few days afterwards, bringing his sister-in-law and niece. This time, he claimed, his sister-in-law and her little girl heard the talking mongoose as well. 'Gef said the name of my sister-in-law's child and said that she had a powder puff in her bag.' He conceded that this was not very telling because both these facts were well-known to Voirrey. Despite that, he remained convinced that Gef was not Voirrey, but 'some extraordinary animal which has developed the power of speech by

some extraordinary process.'

The Northwood visits were the last productive ones for the next three years. But that long timegap did not mean that Gef had gone to earth. On the contrary, the Irvings stated that he became more entertaining and more adventurous during those years. And Jim Irving was able to produce a diary that recorded many of the mongoose's new sayings and antics.

From this account we learn that Gef began killing rabbits to help the family budget. After killing them he would leave them near the house and report the exact position to the family. Then he started bringing home other useful things: a paintbrush one day, then a pair of pincers, then a pair of gloves.

Top: a drawing of Gef from Harry Price's book on the talking mongoose affair. Irving said that he had got the description he gave to the artist from Gef himself, since the mongoose so shyly stayed out of sight

Above: two mongooses in their natural habitat. The Indian species, of which Gef claimed to be one, is famous for its snake-killing skill. But the mongoose is a predator of small mammals as well, and Gef concentrated on killing rabbits

In the house itself, he grew increasingly playful. He would bounce a rubber ball up and down in time with gramophone records and push a lightweight chair around to get exercise. According to the diary, all these events were staged on top of a wooden box-like structure in Voirrey's room, known as 'Gef's Sanctum'.

As a return for his services and entertainment he expected, in fact demanded, choice titbits. For him the orthodox mongoose diet was out. Gef insisted on offerings of lean bacon, sausages, bananas, biscuits, sweets and chocolates. These were carefully placed on one of the crossbeams of the roof so that he could sneak up and grab them when he chose. For Gef continued to be abnormally shy and hated being watched. The family had only brief glimpses of him on rare occasions.

During this period, Gef demonstrated both that he could speak in other languages, even if he used only the odd word and short phrase, and that he could perform some elementary arithmetic. He showed that he could read by yelling out some of the items printed in the newspapers left around the house. He also increased his repertoire of

songs and delighted the family with his renderings of *Home on the range*, *The Isle of Capri* and the Manx national anthem, as well as some Spanish and Welsh ditties.

More surprisingly, Gef allowed himself to be handled – though he still refused to show himself in full. Margaret Irving was permitted to place her finger in his mouth and feel his teeth. She was also graciously allowed to shake one of Gef's paws – which, she said, had 'three long fingers and a thumb'. These paws were obviously extremely versatile, since Irving claimed that Gef had opened drawers with them, struck matches and operated an electric torch.

The irascible Gef grew very free with his insults. When Irving was slow at opening his mail, Gef shouted, 'Read it out you fatheaded gnome!' When a visitor said she was returning to South Africa, he screamed, 'Tell her I hope the propeller drops off!'

A fascinating mystery

The formerly shy and retiring talking mongoose finally even agreed to pose for some photographs taken by Voirrey. But these were of poor quality and revealed almost no details. Then boldness prompted Gef to leave samples of his fur for examination. These samples were forwarded to Captain Macdonald who passed them on to Harry Price. In turn, Price sent them for examination to F. Martin Duncan, an authority on fur and hair at the Zoological Society of London.

While Price waited for the expert's opinion, Captain Macdonald visited Doarlish Cashen once more. Yet again, he heard Gef's voice but saw nothing of the elusive creature. This helped Price to decide to make an inspection of the house himself.

What sealed Price's decision to visit Doarlish Cashen was a revealing report from Duncan on the alleged mongoose hairs. Duncan's letter of 23 April 1935 read:

I have carefully examined them microscopically and compared them with hairs of known origin in my collection. As a result I can definitely state that the specimen hairs never grew upon a mongoose, nor are they those of a rat, rabbit, hare, squirrel or other rodent, or from a sheep, goat or cow. . . .I am inclined to think that these hairs have probably been taken from a longish-haired dog or dogs. . . . When you visit the farm keep a look-out for any dog . . . with a slight curly hair and a fawn and dark colour.

On 30 July 1935 Harry Price trudged up the hill to the Irving home on the trail of the talking mongoose. With him went R.S. Lambert, editor of the *Listener*. The two hoped to solve a fascinating mystery. And they bore Duncan's final words well in mind.

Lost for words

Were Voirrey Irving and Gef, the talking mongoose, one and the same? Were she and her family in a game of deception together? If so, what did they hope to gain?

THE INVESTIGATION BY Harry Price and R.S. Lambert of the talking mongoose of Doarlish Cashen ended after three days, for the amazing Gef failed to speak or display himself. Jim Irving, whose home the creature 'haunted', explained this away by saying that Gef had 'gone missing' some weeks before. So the investigators departed, feeling thwarted and baffled – for the Irvings had seemed to live up to their reputation as level-headed and sincere people.

They left behind a new camera for Irving's daughter Voirrey, but they took away some hairs from the collie dog Mona – samples they had secretly snipped off.

As soon as the two researchers had left the island, Gef reappeared – or so Irving said. And to make up for his temperamental vanishing act, Gef now promised to provide imprints of his paws. Price took up the offer and received three 'paw impressions' made in plasticine. These welcome exhibits were photographed and the prints, marked A, B and C, were given to R.I. Pocock, FRS, at the Natural History Museum in London.

Pocock's opinion of 5 October 1935 was that impression A did not represent the footprint of any animal known to him 'except possibly a raccoon, an American animal'. Impression B had no connection with A, but 'conceivably it was made by a dog'. Impression C had no possible connection with B, for: 'There is no mammal in which there is such disparity in the size of the fore and hind foot.' He concluded: 'I must add that I do not believe these photographs represent foot tracks at all. Most certainly none of them was made by a mongoose.'

Meanwhile, Mona's hair had been given to F. Martin Duncan, who had examined specimens of 'Gef's fur' earlier and had suggested that Price get samples from Voirrey's dog. Duncan's conclusion was unequivocal. He wrote '. . .your sample on examination is absolutely identical with the alleged "mongoose hairs". . .they all came from the same animal – the dog – and not from any "mongoose".' Along with his report, he sent photomicrographs and detailed drawings showing the unmistakable identity of the two batches of hair. So much for the only tangible evidence.

One last visit by Captain Macdonald, who was investigating at Harry Price's request, also failed to provide anything substantially new. Even fresh snapshots by Voirrey were

Right: three paw prints and some teeth marks (bottom right) said to belong to Gef, the talking mongoose of the Isle of Man. A scientist at London's Natural History Museum discredited them

Below right: some of the myriad documents in the file on Gef at the Society for Psychical Research. Gef's antics enlivened the media for several years in the early 1930s

Left: Voirrey and Jim Irving with R.S. Lambert, who investigated their claims about the talking mongoose with Harry Price. Lambert got into trouble with his employer, the BBC, over his part in the matter

Below: the desolate hilltop where the affair of the talking mongoose was played out

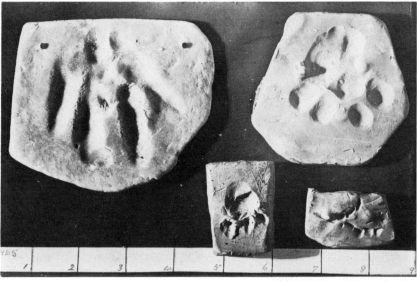

In the end the case just petered out, and the Irvings moved away.

So what lay behind the strange and colourful antics of the talking mongoose? Some of the earliest explanations considered Gef as a psychic phenomenon. The most curious psychical interpretation was advanced by the medium Florence Hodgkin in *Light* magazine of 3 June 1937. She claimed to have received an astonishing communication from a Lama about 'a race of people, actually in existence and living on the Earth at this moment, of whom the world has never heard. They are highly developed, cultured and so advanced that their animals have attained speech.' Gef apparently was an advance emissary, for Florence Hodgkin insisted:

> The Irving family 'know'. . . . That action fought so recently in our Courts of Law [see box] was a means of

of no value, since they simply showed something that could have been an out-of-focus fur collar.

Dr Nandor Fodor was another psychical researcher who looked into the 'Gef' phenomenon thoroughly. At the end of his extensive research on the Isle of Man, he could not come to any conclusion as to what Gef was.

There were four possibilities, as he saw it. One was that Gef was a poltergeist, centring on Voirrey. The second was that Gef was a ghost, haunting the house itself and unconnected to the Irvings. The third was that the elusive animal was a sort of 'familiar', a survival from the days of witchcraft. The final proposition was that Gef was indeed an animal. Fodor reluctantly decided in favour of the animal theory, remarking that 'All the evidence is in favour of Gef being a talking animal. I cannot prove he is an animal. I have not seen him. He did not talk to me. He claimed to be an animal. I cannot disprove that claim.'

Gef permitted Voirrey to take some pictures of him on a five-barred gate, about 300 yards (275 metres) from the house. None of these pictures was of even passable quality though, as Fodor records, 'some of them are distinct enough to show a small animal very much like a mongoose'. The pictures are shadowy and blurred, but a case can be made for Fodor's opinion.

However, the saddest part of the story is that Fodor was given the opportunity to photograph Gef, but he bungled it. What he did was to set up a kitchen scale and train Voirrey's camera at it, with a flashlight so fixed that if Gef could be persuaded to climb on the scale, he would take his own picture. Eventually the mongoose did agree to explode the flash in this way – but the image did not develop properly because of the inexpert way in which the apparatus had been set up. By using make-shift equipment for such an important experiment, Fodor muffed one of the finest opportunities given to a psychic investigator.

B.B.C. HAUNTED

MONGOOSE HAS PUPS ON THE STAIRS

Sir John Reith is ignoring the occurrence in the interests of morality; but it is understood that the first one that talks will be sued for libel.

Thought, word and deed

Richard Stanton Lambert was the editor of the BBC publication the *Listener* at the time that he helped Harry Price to investigate Gef, the talking mongoose – and he came to some grief over his part in the affair. For, after writing about Gef, he found himself under attack by Sir Cecil Levita, a former chairman of the London County Council.

Sir Cecil went to the Assistant Programme Controller at the BBC, Gladstone Murray, and complained about Lambert's involvement in the occult. Words like 'unstable' and 'hysterical' were bandied about with regard to Lambert's character.

Fearing that his job was in jeopardy, Lambert brought a libel action against Sir Cecil. The trial came up on 4 November 1936 and Lambert was represented by the eminent barrister, Sir Patrick Hastings, KC. In summing up the case, Sir Patrick declared, 'Sir Cecil was saying in terms: this man is cracked. He has got to go, and if you, Mr Gladstone Murray, do not yourself go to the BBC and get Mr Lambert removed, I will go to them myself.'

The court found in Lambert's favour and awarded him what were then record damages. But it did not end there. The case caused a sensation and led to questions in Parliament and the setting up of a Parliamentary Board of Enquiry into relationships between the BBC and its staff. This in turn led to reforms within the BBC.

Not bad going for a mongoose – real or imaginary, talking or not.

---

broadcasting in a very real sense this stupendous and unbelievable fact. Irrefutable proof will be forthcoming shortly, because, as the Lama says, 'The time is coming for such a revelation.'

Such a revelation not having come, the talking mongoose affair makes sense only when viewed as a family fantasy.

To understand the background to this case, imagine what it was like living in that sombre, windswept farmhouse. There was no electricity, no television, no radio – not even a next-door neighbour. So the family was thrown in on itself, spending every evening together in gloomy rooms. This probably exaggerated their character traits.

Now, every child lives in a wonderland at times. Many create imaginary playmates who are talked to as if they were flesh and blood. In Voirrey's case, she seems to have created an exotic animal playmate with human capabilities, a mischievous schoolgirl wit, and a moody personality.

But why a mongoose? Well, it so happens that mongooses were once found in the very area that the Irvings lived in. In 1912, a farmer imported dozens of them and let them loose to cut down the rabbit population. That farmer's name was Irvine.

Voirrey could hardly have escaped hearing of *Irvine's* mongooses. And from there it was only one step to thinking about *Irving's* mongoose. Her very own unusual pet. A chatty little creature that would prowl the deadly-dull farmhouse and bring it to life. An exhaustive examination of the documents in this case leads logically to the conclusion that Voirrey and Gef were one and the same. Indeed, one of the earliest newspaper accounts already proposed that the solution to the mystery lay in 'the dual personality' of Voirrey.

Gef never had a personality or existence independent of Voirrey. He brought home rabbits, as did Voirrey. His favourite foods were also Voirrey's favourites. He shared her strong interests in mechanical things. Moreover, Gef was never heard unless Voirrey was out of the room or so placed that her mouth could not be watched. The voice itself was described by one observer, who believed in Gef, as 'like a girl's voice of about 15 or 16 – a striking penetrating voice.' In other words, just the sort of voice Voirrey could easily assume.

It is true that some visitors had difficulty in spotting where Gef's voice came from, but that is not surprising. For the inside walls of the house were covered in boarding to keep out the cold, and these boards were fixed so that they stood some 5 inches (13 centimetres) away from the stone walls. As one reporter observed, 'It cannot be emphasised too much that the interior of the house resembles, in a way, a wooden drum.' Price similarly described the walls as acting like a 'vast speaking tube, with panels like drumheads'. By speaking against these panels, or into one of the many cracks and knotholes, it

Below: Rikki-Tikki-Tavi, the clever and engaging mongoose of Kipling's *The jungle book*. Voirrey Irving was known to be an avid reader of books about animals. If she was Gef's creator, as suspected, maybe she read about, and was inspired by, the storybook mongoose

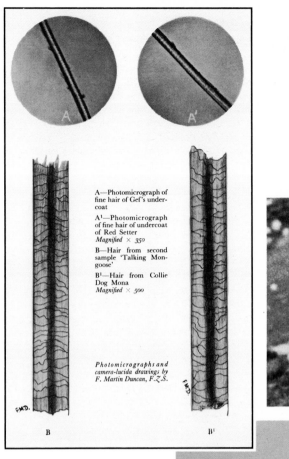

A—Photomicrograph of fine hair of Gef's undercoat

A¹—Photomicrograph of fine hair of undercoat of Red Setter
Magnified × 350

B—Hair from second sample 'Talking Mongoose'

B¹—Hair from Collie Dog Mona
Magnified × 500

Photomicrographs and camera-lucida drawings by F. Martin Duncan, F.Z.S.

B   B¹

Enlarged photographs (top) and detailed drawings (above) showed the sample of 'Gef's fur' (right) to be that of Mona (above right), Voirrey's pet dog. The analysis was made by an expert at the Zoological Society of London

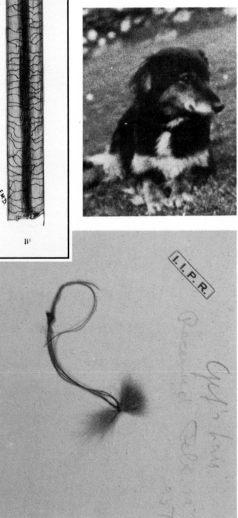

was easy to project the voice and conceal its true point of origin.

But if Voirrey was indeed Gef, why did her parents go along with the deception? It is not unreasonable to assume that they were caught up in the masquerade and became accomplices. Indeed, Jim Irving became so involved that he 'became obsessed with the thing'. He would speak for hours, telling and retelling the saga to anyone who would listen. Price said that Irving spoke about Gef for two hours in his presence and, in that time, his recital 'invariably coincided (almost word for word) with what had been recorded in the letters [he] sent'.

It may well be that Irving came to need the diversion more than Voirrey – to the point of forcing it to continue beyond its natural life. For, as Nandor Fodor noted, appearances in the Irving household were deceptive. Margaret Irving was not the dominant partner she seemed to be. The kingpin of the household was Jim Irving, under whose bland personality Fodor spotted that 'a tyrannical personality arose. . .the family never dared to challenge his autocratic rule.' Fodor summed Irving up as 'a man who failed in life. . . whose passions were too strong to bear this failure with resignation.'

So Irving was a man desperately needing fame of some kind – and promoting Gef made him notorious in his twilight years. Perhaps it was even the high point of his whole life. The publicity, the collecting of anecdotes, the storytelling: all these were Irving's responsibility – and his pride. He constantly interpreted Gef's speech for visitors. Half the time they weren't sure if they had heard the words for themselves or had picked up Irving's translation.

Surprise appearance

His role as an interpreter is clearly shown in the account written for the *Listener* by J. Radcliffe of the *Isle of Man Examiner*. He visited Doarlish Cashen with his father and some friends, but when Gef stayed silent, they left. On the doorstep they chatted for a while. Then:

> Suddenly there was a shrill squeak from the corner of the room where Voirrey, the daughter, was sitting, and Mr Irving in great excitement gripped my arm and pointing to the opposite side of the room whispered: 'He's there! Did you hear him?' Evans and I gazed at each other in sheer amazement. . . . We were again conducted to the door and the squeaks at intermittent intervals continued. Each squeak was kindly translated by Mr Irving to mean: 'They don't believe' or 'I want to back a horse', etc. The squeak in every case was of particularly short duration. . . . On our way down I noticed Voirrey had a tendency to hang behind, and once again we heard a piping squeak with Mr Irving again wildly gesticulating and pointing to the hedge and whispering: 'He's there, I tell you. He's there.' This was really too much, for my hearing is very good, and the squeak without doubt was human and came from immediately behind us. We laughed over the whole incident for days. . .because it was so badly done that it was extremely funny.

And laughter is surely the best response to the 'talking mongoose mystery' – for it was never a malicious affair and it provided a good deal of amusement and excitement. For those who cannot accept this verdict, perhaps Gef himself had the answer when he shrieked: 'Nuts! Put a sock in it! Chew coke!'

The boy with no past

Who was the youth found – bewildered and barely able to speak – in Nuremberg in 1828? Where did he come from? What was his background? GRAHAM FULLER and IAN KNIGHT examine the enigma of Kaspar Hauser

Kaspar Hauser as he first appeared in the streets of Nuremberg in May 1828. No one knew who he was or where he came from. The two letters he carried seemed to offer some clue as to his origins, but subsequent investigation led nowhere

NUREMBERG, SECOND CITY in Germany's fairyland state of Bavaria, was in decline in the early 19th century. The medieval splendour of the days of the Hohenzollens – who had ruled with an iron hand from their castle above the old town – was gone, and the revival brought about by the industrial revolution was yet to come. Nuremberg was a secluded provincial city, yet for five years it was to be the centre of sensation and speculation throughout Europe.

The cause of this excitement was a youth of about 17 years of age, who made his appearance in the city's Unschlitt Square on 26 May 1828. It was Whit Monday, and the day of the annual *Ausflug*, a public holiday. A cobbler, taking his morning constitutional, noticed a youth moving unsteadily in the centre of the street, moaning softly and apparently oblivious of his surroundings. Thinking that the boy might be ill, the cobbler approached him and offered his help. The boy's response was unintelligible, but in his left hand he was clutching an envelope, and the cobbler saw that it was addressed to 'the Captain of the 4th Squadron, 6th Cavalry Regiment'. Intrigued, the cobbler led his new acquaintance to the captain's house, supporting the youth as he staggered and stumbled.

The captain was not at home, but his servant admitted the pair and offered them refreshments. Servant and cobbler alike watched with unabashed curiosity as the youth wolfed bread and water but shied away, as if physically revolted, from meat and beer, all the while staring about him.

'Take care of my child'

When the captain came home, his presence provoked some excitement in the youth, who seemed delighted by his uniform and sword, and kept repeating the words, 'Want to be a soldier like father', 'Don't know' and 'Horse, horse' – which seemed to be the extent of his vocabulary. The envelope he carried proved to contain two letters, neither of which was very enlightening. One purported to be from the boy's mother, giving the date of his birth as 30 April 1812 and exhorting the reader to 'Take care of my child. He has been baptised. His father was a soldier in the 6th Cavalry.' The other, supposedly from a labourer into whose hands the boy had been delivered in October 1812, but written in the same hand as the first, claimed that the writer was afflicted by God with 10 children and could no longer look after this one. It contained the bizarre information that the boy had been brought up since infancy in a locked room, seeing and hearing nothing of his family or the outside world.

The captain questioned the youth but,

receiving no intelligible replies, finally declared that his visitor was 'either a primitive savage or an imbecile', and handed him over to the police as a foundling. The police, however, elicited only the same fractured sentences in answer to their rigorous questioning. Unsure how to proceed, they lodged him in a cell and carefully looked him over. He seemed sturdy enough, and one police officer noted that 'he had a very healthy colour; he did not appear pale or delicate.' The soles of his feet and the palms of his hands were soft, and his feet were also blistered and bleeding. When found, the boy had been wearing a pair of boots that were split at the seams and reinforced with nails and horseshoes, tattered breeches, a jacket that seemed to have been cut from an old frock-coat, and a hat. Nothing offered any clue as to his origins.

The jailer soon noted the behavioural peculiarities of his new charge:

> He can sit for hours without moving a limb. He does not pace the floor, nor does he try to sleep. He sits rigidly without growing in the least uncomfortable. Also, he prefers darkness to light, and can move about in it like a cat.

'Neither insane nor dull-witted'

A doctor called in to examine him suggested that the youth's ability to sit motionless for hours was due to a distortion of his knee joints caused by long periods spent sitting with his legs straight in front of him when young; this in turn accounted for his unsteady gait when walking. The doctor was certain, however, that 'This man is neither insane nor dull-witted, but he has apparently been forcibly prevented in the most disastrous way from attaining any personal or social development.'

Finally someone thought to give the youth a sheet of paper and a pen, with surprising results. He covered the paper with childish lettering, from which only three words emerged: *Reiter* ('cavalryman') and Kaspar Hauser. It was immediately taken that his name was Kaspar Hauser and, although at first he refused to respond to it in any way, he has been known by it ever since.

Kaspar Hauser became an overnight sensation in Nuremberg, the major topic of conversation in a quiet city in holiday mood. Crowds of curious sightseers gathered outside his cell to watch him eat, sleep and defecate without his showing any sign of embarrassment. One of the policemen gave him a small model horse to play with and he was so overjoyed with it that well-wishers soon presented him with half a dozen more. Exposed to a bewildering number of new people, Kaspar began to add to his vocabulary, and within a few weeks he was able to stand before Bürgermeister Binder and members of the town council and give an account of himself. The council published it, in much polished form, as 'Bulletin Number

A rooftop view of Nuremberg in the early 19th century. Fascinated and intrigued by the mysterious Kaspar Hauser, the citizens adopted the boy and entrusted him to Professor George Daumer, the city's finest educationalist

Kaspar Hauser's appearance, seemingly from nowhere, caused great speculation throughout Europe, and rumours abounded as to his origins. One theory was that he was the illegitimate son of Stephanie de Beauharnais, Grand Duchess of Baden (below), and that he had been kept in isolation to avoid a scandal

One' concerning their 'Child of Nuremberg'. He neither knows who he is nor where he came from, for it was only at Nuremberg that he came into the world. He always lived in a hole, where he sat on straw on the ground; he never heard a sound nor saw a vivid light. He awoke and slept and awoke again; when he awoke he found a loaf of bread and a pitcher of water beside him. Sometimes the water tasted nasty, and then he fell asleep again, and when he woke up he found a clean shirt on; he never saw the face of the man who came to him. He had two wooden horses and some ribbons to play with; he was never ill, never unhappy in his hole. . . . One day the man came into his room and put a table over his feet; something white lay on the table, and on this the man made black marks with a pencil which he put in his fingers. This the man did several times and when he was gone Kaspar imitated what he had done. At last he taught him to stand and to walk and finally carried him out of his hole. Of what happened next Kaspar had no very clear idea, until he found himself in Nuremberg with a letter in his hand.

The official bulletin turned Kaspar into a celebrity and his fame spread far beyond the confines of Nuremberg's city walls. Some doubted it all, believing the boy to be a hoaxer and pointing out that Kaspar must have been singularly lacking in curiosity if he had failed to see the face of his guardian at least once in 16 years. Others countered that the man had probably been masked – a suggestion borne out to some extent by subsequent events – and hinted darkly that the boy was the illegitimate son of an aristocratic family, hidden away to prevent a scandal and released only when the conspirators were sure that his identity could not be traced. And traced it was not; the police conducted an exhaustive investigation in and around Nuremberg in an attempt to find Kaspar's 'hole'. Nothing was discovered, and the clues connecting him with the 6th Cavalry led nowhere.

Rather proud of their new and increasingly renowned foundling, the Nuremberg authorities put the boy into the care of Professor George Friedrich Daumer, a noted educationalist and philosopher. To Daumer, Kaspar was the perfect example of the 'feral' child, one who had grown up completely cut off from human contact. The response of such primitives to the outside world was the subject of much discussion among scientists of the day, and Daumer kept careful note of Kaspar's reactions.

Certainly his animal senses were extremely well-developed. His hearing was sharp. He could see in the dark and had apparently taken some time to accustom

Right: Castle Pilsach, which some have suggested was the childhood home of Kaspar Hauser. It is thought that Kaspar was kept in a small windowless – or permanently shuttered – room in the castle, and was tended by its caretaker, Franz Richter. When Richter's wife died, he no longer felt able to look after the boy and sent him to Nuremberg

Notes and drawings made by Kaspar Hauser during his tutelage under Professor Daumer. Kaspar learned to read and write very quickly, but this only furthered the controversy about his origins: those who believed him to be of noble birth claimed that, had Kaspar been a peasant boy, he would not have achieved so much in such a short time; the sceptics stated that his progress could be regarded as perfectly normal

himself to bright light. Most acute was his sense of smell. Once he had identified a particular animal's scent, he could track it with ease – a faculty that enabled him to recognise humans in the dark. He could even distinguish trees by the scent of their leaves.

Daumer noted that Kaspar had no idea about the fundamentals of science that govern everyday life. He seemed unable to distinguish between animate and inanimate objects, and was convinced that a ticking grandfather clock was alive, refusing to go near it. When confronted with a mirror he looked behind it to find the owner of the face staring at him. He attempted to pick the flame from the tip of a burning piece of waxed paper – and cried when it burned him. He expected animals to behave in the same way as humans, and believed that balls bounced because they wanted to jump.

Yet Kaspar was not otherwise slow to learn. Daumer was a gifted man and he obtained excellent results from his pupil. Kaspar showed himself to be surprisingly intelligent and possessed of a seemingly

photographic memory, which seldom let him forget a face. He learned to read, write and articulate, and some of his surviving notes include finely executed drawings.

Furthermore, Kaspar Hauser revelled in the attention that came his way after so much social deprivation. For the best part of a year he was Nuremberg's most fêted celebrity, the star personality in fashionable drawing-room conversation. Visitors called to see him regularly and he was frequently invited out. His case is not dissimilar to that of John Merrick, the deformed 'elephant man' whose tragedy made him as great a celebrity with Victorian society as Kaspar's mysterious origins made him with the Nuremberg gentry. Opinions concerning those origins polarised. The people who believed his story now openly linked him with the ruling family of Bavaria, suggesting that he was the bastard son of the Grand Duchess of Baden. To support their claim they cited Daumer's achievements in Kaspar's education. No peasant boy could have learned so much so quickly and, besides, why would any peasant family go to such trouble to hide his origins?

Many, however, were sceptical of such theories. They took Kaspar's introductory letters at face value, declaiming that the behaviour of a peasant family over-stocked with children need not be rationalised. They pointed to the rough clothes Kaspar was wearing when discovered, and suggested that his progress seemed remarkable only in the light of his previous history. In an ordinary child such achievements would pass unnoticed. Some still believed the whole thing a hoax, that Kaspar's idiosyncrasies had been exaggerated, and that his early inarticulacy was due to his being a foreign vagrant.

To state his case further, and to quieten his detractors, Kaspar Hauser sat down with Professor Daumer in the summer of 1829 and wrote his autobiography.

Who was Kaspar Hauser?

Left: Bruno S as Kaspar Hauser in Werner Herzog's film, which was made in 1975. The enigmatic foundling is still a source of fascination, and numerous books have been written about him – yet his true identity has never been established

Below: the first attempt on Kaspar's life, at the home of his guardian Dr Daumer. The masked assailant struck Kaspar then fled, leaving the boy unconscious in the cellar

As Kaspar Hauser's fame spread, investigators doubled their efforts to piece together his background. But just as the puzzle seemed to be solved, Kaspar was brutally murdered. Who killed him – and why?

KASPAR HAUSER'S AUTOBIOGRAPHY, when it appeared in August 1829, proved something of a disappointment to the people of Nuremberg. It revealed nothing new about his background, but merely gave a more detailed account of his life in confinement, a story already widely known – and in some cases embellished by popular rumour to the extent that the facts seemed decidedly dull in comparison.

If the public felt at all cheated, however, it did not have long to wait for a new sensation. On 7 October 1829 Kaspar was found prostrate in Dr Daumer's cellar with a wound in his forehead. He was carried upstairs and put to bed, but little about the incident emerged beyond the fact that he had been hit by a man with 'a black face', which was taken to mean a man with a mask.

Nuremberg was aghast, taking the assault as proof that Kaspar had enemies in high places who were disturbed by the publication of his life story, and who feared it would let some secret slip. Anxious to avoid another attack on their most famous son, the town

council moved Kaspar to an undisclosed address and provided a police guard. For two years the boy was surrounded only by his champions, but the novelty of supporting a celebrity on their taxes began to lose its appeal to the people of Nuremberg and several citizens complained about the cost.

Fortunately a solution was to hand. An English aristocrat, Lord Stanhope, had taken an interest in the case and wanted to adopt the youth. Nuremberg's councillors were prepared to allow Stanhope to assume temporary custody of Kaspar in return for a contribution towards his upkeep. Stanhope, who seems to have regarded the boy as an unusual toy with which to amuse his friends, then took him on a tour of Europe and presented him at the courts of various minor principalities and kingdoms. It does not appear to have been a complete success, novel entertainment though Kaspar undoubtedly was, and certain members of the Bavarian royal house threatened law suits if their name continued to be linked with his. Meanwhile, Kaspar and Stanhope, wilful foundling and eccentric Englishman, began to quarrel. Finally, in 1833, Stanhope applied to the Nuremberg Council for permission to lodge Kaspar permanently in the town of Ansbach some 25 miles (40 kilometres) away, in the care of his friend Dr Meyer. The Nurembergers were reluctant to sever the tie completely, but Stanhope's influence was considerable and eventually they agreed.

Kaspar's tutelage began anew with Meyer. The doctor had him confirmed in the Protestant Church and attempted to school him in Latin and history as well as practical subjects. Kaspar did not thrive; he became introspective and moody, and seems to have

Below: the fatal attack on Kaspar Hauser, as portrayed in Herzog's film. Kaspar managed to stagger home, but died from his wounds three days later, on 17 December 1833

resented the way Meyer treated him. No longer the centre of a crowd of admirers, he may well have simply refused to learn. Meyer pronounced in disgust that Kaspar's mental abilities had been grossly exaggerated and that he had the mind of an eight-year-old. Stanhope's interest began to fade.

Kaspar himself longed to return to Nuremberg and to the friends and supporters he had left behind there. He made one brief visit in 1833, which further fuelled this desire – but events overtook him.

On 14 December 1833 Kaspar Hauser

staggered into Dr Meyer's house clutching his side. Gasping 'Man stabbed! Knife! Park! Gave wallet! Go quick!', he collapsed to the floor in a pool of blood.

For several days the people of Nuremberg and Ansbach held their breath. Kaspar lay seriously ill, the knife having entered the left side of his chest, damaging his lungs and liver. He did manage to reveal some details of the attack. A stranger – 'tall, with dark whiskers and a black coat' – had approached him and asked, 'Are you Kaspar Hauser?' When told that he was, the man promised to give information about the boy's family and led him to Ansbach's city park where he handed him a wallet. When Kaspar opened it the man stabbed him and ran off.

The police moved rapidly to catch the assailant, but he could not be traced. The wallet was found where Kaspar had dropped it, but all it contained was an enigmatic note. Written back to front, to be read in a mirror, it said:

Hauser will be able to tell you how I look, whence I came from and who I am. To spare him the task, I will tell you myself. I am from . . . on the Bavarian border . . . on the river. . . . My name is MLO.

Death of an enigma

The nonsensical nature of this message led some to believe that Kaspar had fabricated the attack. Captain Hickel of the Ansbach police questioned the boy as he lay wounded, but all he would say was, 'I didn't do it myself.' These were to be his last words. The wound set up complications, and on 17 December 1833 Kaspar Hauser died.

The public, throughout Bavaria, was outraged, and large rewards were offered for any information concerning the identity of the assassin. None was forthcoming. When huge crowds followed Kaspar's body as it was taken to its last resting place, they saw it buried beneath a headstone that ably summed up his life: 'Here lies Kaspar Hauser, the riddle of his time. His birth was unknown, his death mysterious.'

The strange circumstances of his murder strike right at the heart of the mystery that surrounds Kaspar Hauser. His last guardian, Dr Meyer, was convinced that the boy had inflicted the wound on himself to attract attention, possibly with an eye to getting himself returned to Nuremberg, but that the dagger had done rather more damage than Kaspar had expected. Certainly there were no witnesses to either of the attacks upon Kaspar, and both wounds could have been self-inflicted. It was reported that police investigating the scene of the fatal assault scoured the Ansbach gardens but found no footprints other than Kaspar's. And the timing, too, may have been significant. The first attack took place following the disappointment of Kaspar's autobiography, which it soon overshadowed, and the second attack

occurred when his fame was beginning to wane – instantly, and ironically, bringing his name into the limelight once more.

But perhaps Kaspar's enemies wanted him dead. Many of his friends argued that he was the victim of a conspiracy. Someone with something to hide, they said, had ordered the first attack to cast doubts on his credibility, or more likely to warn him to keep his mouth shut; with the second they silenced him forever. If the attacks were linked, they suggest a motivating party with enough influence – and reason – to have Kaspar followed over a period of four years and then eliminated. The assault in Daumer's house could have been a bungled murder attempt, the would-be assassin panicking and fleeing when Kaspar cried out. Since Kaspar was seldom left alone, his killer would have had to wait perhaps years to find the right moment to strike, which could partly explain the great length of time between the attacks. If the motive of the murder had been to silence Kaspar, then it is also worth considering that several prominent Nurembergers, including Bürgermeister Binder, died in mysterious circumstances in the years following Kaspar's death. What had Kaspar told them?

'Citizen of another planet'

Lastly, there is the possibility that Kaspar Hauser was murdered by the man who had raised him, whoever that might have been. Kaspar's descriptions of his assailants were vague, but the masked man who tended to him in childhood might easily have been the same man with 'a black face' who attacked him at Daumer's house, or the man 'with dark whiskers and a black coat' who finished him off. If so, motivation is harder to find: if Kaspar came from a family of no particular note, why should the man have felt the need first to release him and then to kill him? And what was the significance of the bizarre

Top: the monument marking the spot where Kaspar was stabbed in Ansbach park

Above: the last resting place of Kaspar Hauser, 'the riddle of his time. His birth was unknown, his death mysterious'

murder note? Did it have a meaning in the eyes of a royally paid assassin, or of an ex-soldier of the 6th Cavalry? Or was it purely intended to throw the police off the track? No rational motive can easily be found, although of course murder is not always a rational business.

All the unknown quantities concerning Kaspar Hauser's brief life, and the five years he spent in the public eye, have continued to fascinate investigators. The original accounts of his appearance and behaviour have been meticulously studied, and inconsistencies exaggerated beyond all importance. A comment by Anselm von Feuerbach, a patron in Ansbach, has even been taken as proof of an extra-terrestrial connection:

> Kaspar Hauser showed such an utter deficiency of words and ideas, such perfect ignorance of the commonest things and appearances of Nature, and such a horror of all customs, conveniences and necessities of civilised life, and, withal, such extraordinary peculiarities in his social, mental and physical disposition, that one might feel one's self driven to the alternative of believing him to be a citizen of another planet, transferred by some miracle to our own.

Kaspar Hauser's life has been the subject of books, novels, plays and a film (Werner Herzog's *The enigma of Kaspar Hauser*, made in 1975), each with its own contribution to make to the nature of the mystery.

But the question remains: who *was* Kaspar Hauser?

The terror of London

Who was the frightening figure – a man known only as Spring-heeled Jack – who terrorised the people of London for decades in the 19th century? In an attempt to unravel the mystery PAUL BEGG **examines the legend that has built up around this bizarre character**

THE LONELY LANES AND COMMONS of 19th-century suburban London were haunted by the weird and terrifying figure of Spring-heeled Jack, who pounced upon passers-by, sometimes wounded them severely, and bounded away in enormous leaps. Today the antics of Spring-heeled Jack are almost forgotten, or dismissed as a figment of the imagination – a mere character in Victorian horror literature, or a bogeyman used by mothers to warn errant children: 'Be good or Spring-heeled Jack will get you!' Some writers believe that Jack is a figure of popular folklore. Kellow Chesney in his book *The Victorian underworld* says that Jack is 'pure legend' – perhaps the invention of servants reluctant to admit negligence when thieves robbed their master's home.

But Jack was not a character in fiction, folklore or legend. He was real, and his appearances were widely reported in the local and national press.

Nobody seems certain when Jack first appeared. Many sources say that reports of a peculiar leaping man were in circulation as early as 1817, but it was not until 1838 that Spring-heeled Jack became a figure of considerable and widespread interest and speculation. On 9 January 1838 the Lord Mayor of London, Alderman Sir John Cowan, revealed, at a public session held in the Mansion House, the contents of a letter he had received several days earlier. He had withheld it, he said, in the hope of obtaining further information. The correspondent, who signed the letter 'a resident of Peckham', wrote that, as the result of a wager, a person of the highest rank had adopted several frightening guises and set out to scare 30 people to death. He had 'already succeeded in depriving seven ladies of their senses', two of whom 'were not likely to recover, but likely to become burdens to their families.' The resident of Peckham continued:

> The affair has now been going on for some time, and, strange to say, the papers are still silent on the subject. The writer has reason to believe that they have the whole history at their finger-ends but, through interested motives, are induced to remain silent.

We do not know why the Lord Mayor made

the contents of this letter public, nor can we judge the truth of the letter's allegation of a press 'cover-up', but from the quantity of letters that poured into the Mansion House it is clear that the activities of Spring-heeled Jack were common knowledge in suburban London.

Spring-heeled Jack had appeared as a milk-white bull, a white bear, and an enormous baboon; he had been seen dressed in a suit of shining brass armour, and on another occasion in one of burnished steel; once, in Hackney, he appeared as a lamplighter – who walked upon his hands and carried his ladder between his feet. His ability to make prodigious leaps was popularly ascribed to springs attached to his boots.

On Wednesday, 18 February 1838, 18-year-old Lucy Scales and her sister Margaret were returning home after visiting their brother, a butcher who lived in a respectable part of the district of Limehouse. Lucy, slightly ahead of her sister, was passing the

Above: Tod Slaughter as Spring-heeled Jack in the spine-chilling film *The curse of the Wraydons*, which was made in 1946

Left: 'Spring-heeled Jack parts the lovers', an illustration from a 19th-century 'penny dreadful'. Jack was the inspiration for several of these weekly serials: although usually portrayed as the villain of the piece, often terrorising young women (far left), he occasionally appeared as the hero, an avenger of crime and a punisher of wrong-doers (below left)

entrance to Green Dragon Alley when a figure leapt upon her from the shadows. The apparition breathed fire into Lucy's face and then bounded away as the girl fell to the ground, seized by violent fits.

Two days later, 18-year-old Jane Alsop replied to a violent ringing of the bell at the front gate of her parents' home in east London. Outside was an extremely agitated man who identified himself as a policeman. 'For God's sake bring me a light,' he cried, 'for we have caught Spring-heeled Jack in the lane!'

Blinded by fire

Jane fetched a candle, but when she handed it to the 'policeman', the man discarded his all-enveloping cloak. On his head was a large helmet, he wore a skin-tight suit of what looked like white oilskin, and in the light of the candle his protuberant eyes burned like coals. Without uttering a word, he vomited blue and white flames into Jane's face and grabbed the temporarily blinded and very frightened girl with talon-like fingers, which tore her dress and raked her skin. Attracted by her screams, Jane's sisters, Mary and Sarah, came to the girl's assistance. Somehow Sarah pulled Jane from the fiend's grasp, thrust her indoors and slammed the door in Jack's face.

A week later Jack tried the same deception but for some reason his intended victim was suspicious and Jack was forced to flee. A witness claimed that under his cloak Jack had been wearing an ornate crest and, in gold filigree, the letter 'w'.

After these attacks Jack's infamy grew. His exploits were reported in many newspapers and became the subject of no less than four 'penny dreadfuls' and melodramas performed in the cheap theatres that abounded at that time. But, perhaps as a result of the publicity, Jack's appearances became less

The man who created life

Out of his test tubes and retorts, Andrew Crosse is said to have created living creatures – and so threw his 19th-century world into a frenzy. PAUL BEGG asks if this English gentleman-scientist was a real-life Frankenstein

FEAR HANGS OVER the village as heavy and black as the threatening storm-clouds. In the distance a sprawling mansion stands gaunt against the hills. A dim yellow light from a ground floor window shows that the scientist is at home and at work. A roll of thunder echoes around the hills. A flash of lightning rends the sky. Suddenly the mansion window is ablaze with stark, almost incandescent light. The fear tightens as the villagers imagine the demonic activities that could be going on inside the grey, forbidding walls of the mansion.

This description could fit the popular image of Baron Victor Frankenstein at work, but it could be applied equally to a real-life gentleman-scientist named Andrew Crosse. He too had a compulsion towards unorthodox laboratory experiments and is said to have actually created life from inanimate matter.

Andrew Crosse was born into a wealthy English family on 17 June 1784. In 1793 he was sent to Dr Seyer's School in The Fort in Bristol, and it was here that he was introduced to science.

Later described by his second wife as one who 'delighted in whatever was strange and

Benjamin Franklin, American political leader and diplomat, writer and scientist. Crosse probably heard about Franklin's own electrical experiments through his father, who was a personal acquaintance

marvellous', Crosse was obsessed with the new science of electricity from about the age of 12. It is possible that his interest was inspired by his father, among whose acquaintances were Benjamin Franklin and Joseph Priestley, two pioneers of the new science. Crosse himself attributed it to a lecture on the subject. In any event, he spent much of his time thereafter conducting experiments.

In June 1802 he went to Brasenose College, Oxford. Here he was encouraged to lead a profligate life and he virtually abandoned his experiments.

Crosse inherited the family estates and fortune in 1805 on the death of his mother and teetered on the brink of becoming a typical wealthy wastrel, until he met George John Singer at a party. Singer's great passion for electrical experiments rekindled Crosse's own enthusiasm and in 1807 he began a series of experiments into electro-crystallisation at Fyne Court, his family seat.

In 1837 one of Crosse's experiments resulted in something that has puzzled scientists to this day. From inanimate matter Andrew Crosse created life. He tells how it happened:

In the course of my endeavours to form artificial minerals by a long continued electric action on fluids holding in solution such substances as were necessary to my purpose, I had recourse to every variety of contrivance that I could think of; amongst others I constructed a wooden frame, which supported a Wedgewood funnel, within which rested a quart basin on a circular piece of mahogany. When this basin was filled with a fluid, a strip of flannel wetted with the same was suspended over the side of the basin and inside the funnel, which, acting as a syphon, conveyed the fluid out of the basin through the funnel in successive drops: these drops fell into a smaller funnel of glass placed beneath the other, and which contained a piece of somewhat porous red oxide iron from Vesuvius. This stone was kept constantly electrified. . . .

On the fourteenth day from the commencement of this experiment I observed through a lens a few small whitish excrescences or nipples, projecting from about the middle of the electrified stone. On the eighteenth day these projections enlarged, and stuck out seven or eight filaments, each of them longer than the hemisphere on which they grew. On the twenty-sixth day these appearances assumed the form of a perfect insect, standing erect on a few bristles which formed its tail. . . . On the twenty-eighth day these little creatures moved their legs. . . . After a few days they detached themselves from the stone, and moved about at pleasure.

Crosse was baffled by this totally unexpected development. He anxiously sought a rational explanation but none seemed available. Over the succeeding months he repeated the experiment. He then wrote:

After many months' action and consequent formation of certain crystalline matters, I observed similar excrescences with those before described at the edge of the fluid in every one of the cylinders except two which contained the carbonate of potassa and the metallic arsenic; and in due time the whitish

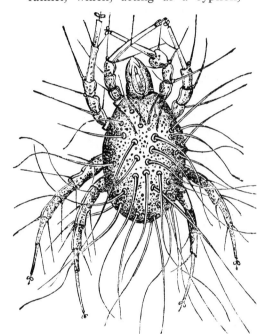

The strange insect that came to life in the bottom of a basin during Crosse's experiments with electricity. Crosse was reviled by the religious community for meddling in God's work when the existence of the 'acari' came to light

Fyne Court, the family seat of Andrew Crosse. Here he carried out his many experiments – for a long time in secret – and gave rise to the local opinion that he was probably an evil wizard

appearances were developed into insects. In my first experiment I had made use of flannel, wood, and a volcanic stone. In the last, none of these substances were present.

Again no solution presented itself for the appearance of these acari, or tiny mites, and he repeated the experiment a third time. On this occasion Crosse made an error that, far from shedding any light on the mystery, merely served to intensify it:

I had omitted to insert within the bulb of the retort a resting place for these acari (they are always destroyed if they fall back into the fluid from which they have emerged). It is strange that, in a solution eminently caustic and under an atmosphere of oxihydrogen gas, one single acarus should have made its appearance.

The discovery made public

Andrew Crosse now wrote a report on his 'discovery' and dispatched it to the Electrical Society in London. It was received with some scepticism but sufficient interest to invite another electrical experimenter to repeat Crosse's work. The man chosen for the task was W.H. Weeks of Sandwich in Kent. The results were published in the *Annals of Electricity* (October 1836–1837) and in the *Transactions* of the London Electrical Society (1838).

Weeks published only a summary of the results of his experiments, but it seems clear that he took a number of precautions to ensure that no extraneous matter, such as the ova of insects, had in some manner gained entry into his equipment. Weeks worked slowly and methodically. While he was still experimenting, the story of Crosse's discovery became public knowledge.

Had the matter been confined to the

Right: the frontispiece of *Noad's lectures on electricity*, in which detailed descriptions of Crosse's experiments were published. Crosse's name appears on the top left of the arch above the title, along with other illustrious scientists

Below: the scientist Michael Faraday at work in his laboratory. This respected physicist and chemist was a defender of Crosse during the controversy surrounding his experiments

scientific community, it is probable that it would not have caused the storm that it did. But Crosse discussed the acari, to which he had apparently given life, with a number of friends. One of these was the editor of the *Western Gazette*. Crosse's second wife, Cornelia, recorded the result:

. . . the editor of a West of England paper . . . immediately, unauthorised, but in a very friendly spirit, published an account of the experiment; which account quickly flew over England, and indeed Europe, satisfying at once the credulity of those who love the marvellous, and raising up a host of bitter and equally unreasoning assailants, whose personal attacks on Mr Crosse, and their misrepresentations of his views, were at once ridiculous and annoying.

As the storm broke and whirled around Andrew Crosse, many people came to his defence. Among them was the respected scientist Michael Faraday who, in an impassioned lecture at the Royal Institution in 1837, condemned those who attacked Crosse. Faraday also claimed to have conducted Crosse's experiment himself and to have confirmed Crosse's findings. However, this did nothing to lessen the controversy and neither did Mr Weeks, who confirmed that Crosse's experiment did indeed 'give birth' to the acari. In fact, it could be argued that Faraday and Weeks unintentionally intensified the widespread opinion that Crosse was a meddler in the act of creation, a man who set himself up as a rival of God.

Andrew Crosse was angered, hurt,

possibly mystified by the outburst, and he retired to the seclusion of Fyne Court. Here he found himself reviled and shunned by his neighbours. On one occasion a local clergyman, the Reverend Philip Smith, conducted a service of exorcism on the hills above Crosse's country estate.

In 1846 Crosse's first wife and his brother Richard died within four days of each other. Bereaved, Crosse returned to his experiments. In his journal and in letters to friends he wrote of his hopes and aspirations. He said that he wanted to construct 'a battery at once cheap, powerful and durable' – perhaps a vision of the dry-cell battery that was patented by Georges Leclanché in 1868. He also experimented with the preservation of food and the purification of sea water and other liquids through the use of electricity.

A new lease of life

In the late 1840s Andrew Crosse emerged from his self-imposed seclusion at Fyne Court. In 1849 he met Cornelia Burns, still in her twenties, and romance blossomed. Crosse took on a new lease of life and even began attending a few social gatherings. On 22 July 1850 the two were married.

Over the next five years Crosse's health began to deteriorate and on 26 May 1855 he suffered a paralytic seizure. He never recovered. On 6 July he awoke in terrible pain. Holding his young wife's hand just before dying, he said, 'My dear, the utmost extent of human knowledge is but comparative ignorance.'

Today Andrew Crosse is all but forgotten, just one of the many amateur scientists who in some small way contributed to the widening of scientific knowledge. Where his name is remembered, it is not in scientific textbooks but in books about mysteries.

The question remains: what were the acari? Nobody in recent years has been known to repeat Crosse's experiment, and no solution to the mystery seems to be generally accepted. Several theories have, however, been proposed.

Dr A.C. Oudemans in 1934 suggested that

Right: a giant insect is about to attack in the story *The electric vampire*, which appeared in the *London Magazine* in 1910. It was inspired by the tales about how Crosse had created life in his laboratory in an insect-like form

Below: Mary Shelley, author of *Frankenstein*. Crosse in many ways lived up to the popular image of the man she made famous in one of the best-known horror tales in all literature

Left: Crosse's grave stone. The inscription refers to him as 'the electrician' – a modest designation for a man whose intricate experiments and slightly odd character made him a storm centre

the acari were *Glyophagus domesticus*, a commonplace insect that has an amazing power to hold onto life no matter what the conditions. It also manages to get into equipment despite precautions to keep it out.

Another idea is that the chemical constituents in Crosse's tests took on a form and gave the appearance of living things.

Perhaps one of these theories could be correct. But it is difficult to credit that the ova of *Glyophagus domesticus* were present in all the experiments conducted by Crosse, Weeks and possibly Faraday. It is likewise hard to believe that the experimenters did not consider and test the possibility that the acarus was not a living creature.

In the final analysis, we do not know what Andrew Crosse's acari were – and the man himself remains strange and extraordinary.

In his book *The man who was Frankenstein*, Peter Haining suggests that Crosse was the model for Mary Shelley's Baron Frankenstein. He points out that, in the autumn of 1814, the Shelleys were visited by the poet Robert Southey, who knew Crosse and had stayed at Fyne Court. The three apparently discussed Crosse's electrical experiments and on 28 December, Mary and Percy Shelley attended a lecture given by Crosse.

The evidence that Andrew Crosse and his experiments with the new science of electricity fuelled Mary Shelley's imagination is at best circumstantial. But this slightly eccentric gentleman-scientist, experimenting in his remote mansion in the wilds of the hazy Quantocks, certainly fits the popular picture of Baron Victor Frankenstein.

Turning in the grave

The mysterious movement of lead-cased coffins in a sealed tomb in Barbados in the 19th century was believed by many to be the work of some supernatural force. What really happened? GRAHAM FULLER and IAN KNIGHT report

THEY SAY the dead tell no tales. And since the corpses interred in a Barbadian graveyard vault early last century were, apparently, the only human agencies present when the actual coffins they were laid in moved, there naturally exists no immediate first-hand account of this eeriest of mysteries.

The so-called 'creeping coffins of Barbados' crept, with some alacrity, into West Indian folklore between 1812 and 1820. Indeed, this was no isolated incident, but a phenomenon that repeated itself with chilling regularity until the nerve of the vault's owners and the local dignitaries finally ran out. At the time the tomb in question, situated near the entrance of the graveyard of Christ Church, overlooking the bay at Oistins on the south coast of the island, belonged to the Chase family. It was a solid affair, built of large, cemented blocks of coral, 12 feet long by 6 feet wide (4 metres by 2 metres), sunk halfway into the ground and sealed off by a great marble slab. Anyone trying secretly to get in (or out) of the vault would have found it an arduous task.

Two burials took place before anything happened. On 31 July 1807 Mrs Thomasina Goddard's funeral was held, and on 22 February 1808 that of the infant Mary Anna Maria Chase. Then, on 6 July 1812, pallbearers and mourners arrived to lay to rest Dorcas Chase, the elder sister of Mary Anna Maria. Several of the men heaved the door open – struggling with its great weight – and the coffin was lifted down to the portals of the tomb. Peering into the darkness from the few first steps, the leading pallbearers were greeted by a truly sepulchral sight. Mary Anna Maria's coffin had moved to the corner opposite the one in which it had been placed; Mrs Goddard's had been flung aside against a wall. Something more than a draught had moved them – both coffins were cased in lead. Without pausing to ask questions the labourers lifted them back into position, placed Dorcas's among them and sealed the vault up again. But who or what had tampered with the dead – and why? Amazed and frightened, the mourners chose to put the blame on the Negro slaves who had assisted at the funeral of the first Chase sister.

So were the Negroes to blame? There was reputedly little love lost between the patriarch Thomas Chase and the black slaves he employed. Chase was by all accounts a cruel man whose tyrannical behaviour had driven his daughter Dorcas to kill herself. It seems improbable though that anyone bearing a grudge against him would have gone to such lengths to inflict such trivial damage.

The work of malign spirits?

As it was, Chase himself died within the month; and on 9 August 1812 his coffin was placed among the other three, which this time had remained undisturbed. A few years slipped by with no reason for anyone to believe that anything untoward was taking place in the Oistins churchyard. On 25 September 1816 the vault was reopened for the burial of a little boy, Samuel Brewster Ames. Once again the coffins lay in disarray – and the accusing eye was again turned on the Negro labourers, who promptly denied all charges and shrank in fear from what they considered the work of malign spirits: Negroes regarded the dead with superstition and were in fact the most unlikely of suspects. There was little the mourners could do, however, but return the coffins to their rightful places, leave Master Ames among them and block up the doorway with the great slab – which they did, hastily. It was opened again on 17 November for the interment of Samuel Brewster, whose coffin was being transferred to the Chase vault from its original home in a St Philip graveyard. The mystery surrounding the vault was now so

well-known that a crowd gathered in antici-
pation of fresh disturbances.

It was not to be disappointed. All of the
coffins had shifted ground. That of Mrs
Goddard, who had been lying in 'rest' now
for nearly a decade, had finally given up
under the strain and fallen apart. An exhaustive search of the vault proved futile –
the walls, floor and roof were as solid and
unyielding as ever. And yet for the third time
there were unmistakable signs of violent
activity within. Would it happen again? One
wonders with what sense of dreadful,
resigned foreboding the mourners reposi-
tioned the coffins (tying and bundling the
remnants of Mrs Goddard's against the wall)
and cemented the great door back into place.

Nearly three years passed before the vault
was opened again – during which time it
received thousands of curious visitors. On 17
July 1819 the funeral of Thomasina Clarke
took place. It seems that the mystery was
now a major national issue, for Viscount
Combermere, the Governor of Barbados,
and two of his officials attended the funeral.
In front of hundreds of hushed spectators the
marble slab was cut free by masons and
dragged aside by a team of slaves. Inside, all
was chaos; every coffin had moved save only
the shattered fragments of Mrs Goddard's,
which had remained in their little pile. The
vault was searched again. Nothing. Not one
clue. Undeterred, the labourers lugged the
coffins back. Sand was then sent for and
sprinkled over the floor of the tomb so that it
formed a smooth, thick carpet that would
surely show the traces of the mysterious
coffin mover. Once the door was replaced

The bay at Oistins on the
south coast of Barbados
received thousands of
visitors in the years between
1812 and 1820. The tourists
flocked to Christ Church
graveyard to see at first hand
the vault of the Chase family
where, it was rumoured,
someone – or something –
was tampering with the dead

Combermere left the impression of his seal
in the cement and others did the same.

No recently deceased Barbadian was
brought to the vault when it was opened
again on 18 April 1820. Public speculation
and excitement about the strange goings-on
had mounted to such a degree that no one had
the patience to wait for someone to pass on
before the mystery could be finally solved or
abandoned. After prolonged debate that
could lead to only one conclusion, Viscount
Combermere, the Honourable Nathan
Lucas, Major J. Finch (secretary to the
Governor), Mr R. Bowcher Clarke and Mr
Rowland Cotton journeyed to Christ
Church, collected the Reverend Thomas
Orderson and repaired to the graveyard with
a band of quaking Negro labourers.

The seals on the cement were intact – no
one had therefore since removed the door
and entered that way. And from the outside
the vault was as solid as ever. Combermere
ordered the cement to be chipped away and
the huge slab was dragged aside, causing a
strange, grating noise. This was the result of
one of the larger lead coffins having been
thrown up against the door, against which it
now lay. Mary Anna Maria's tinier coffin,
meanwhile, had been sent flying to the far
end of the vault with such violence that it had
damaged the coral wall. The other coffins

were scattered about, but there were no tell-tale marks in the sand to suggest what might have moved them. The Honourable Nathan Lucas, reporting the incident, had this to say:

> I examined the walls, the arch, and every part of the vault, and found every part old and similar; and a mason in my presence struck every part of the bottom with his hammer, and all was solid. I confess myself at a loss to account for the movements of these leaden coffins. Thieves certainly had no hand in it; and as for any practical wit or hoax, too many were requisite to be trusted with the secret for it to remain unknown; and as for negroes having anything to do with it, their superstitious fear of the dead and everything belonging to them precludes any idea of the kind. All I know is that it happened and that I was an eye-witness of the fact!!!

Whatever, or whoever, it was that caused the coffins in the Chase vault to wander between those four walls was given no further opportunity to do so. All of the coffins were lugged out and given more peaceful resting places elsewhere in the churchyard. The vault remains open and unused to this day.

'Werewolves and vampires'

There have been other cases of coffins refusing to stay put. Discussing the Barbados mystery in his book *West Indian tales of old*, Sir Algernon E. Aspinall makes reference to the *European Magazine* of September 1815, which cites a vault at Stanton in Suffolk, England, where on at least three separate occasions, and, as at Oistins, behind a sealed door, coffins had moved off their raised biers; during one of these 'manoeuvres' the heaviest coffin – another eight-pallbearer affair – had climbed onto the fourth step of the vault. 'Whence arose this operation, in which it was certain that no-one had a hand?' asked the *European Magazine* writer. Needless to say, the people of Stanton were as shocked as the Barbadians. In 1867 Mr F. C. Paley, son of the rector of Gretford, near Stamford in Lincolnshire, England, wrote to *Notes and Queries* concerning the repeated movement of heavy lead coffins (also cased in wood) in a local vault; his letter was corroborated by a witness who commented that some of the coffins had moved to a leaning position against the wall.

The superstitious people of Arensburg on the Baltic island of Oesel immediately blamed vampires and werewolves when similar trouble occurred in the town cemetery in 1844. The crisis started in June with the 'spooking' of horses belonging to visitors to the graveyard. Some of these horses bolted, others fainted or dropped dead; many, so the story goes, went mad. The fault was laid at the door of the Buxhoewden family vault. When a funeral service in the family chapel was interrupted by eerie sounds from the

The entrance to the Chase vault in Christ Church graveyard, Oistins. The vault has stood open and empty since 1820, when all the coffins it contained were removed and buried in another, more peaceful, place

Viscount Combermere, the Governor of Barbados, supervised the sealing of the Chase vault after the funeral of Thomasina Clarke on 17 July 1819. When he returned nine months later to check on the state of the tomb he found the coffins in total disarray – and yet the seals on the door had remained intact

adjacent burial chamber, the bravest of the Buxhoewdens entered the tomb to find that the coffins of their late relatives had been thrown around. Rumours of 'devilry' spread and there was great fear and consternation in Arensburg. The president of the local ecclesiastical court, the Baron de Guldenstabbé, headed an official enquiry and personally visited the vault, which had been put back in order and locked. The coffins had moved again.

Determined to get to the bottom of the mystery, the Baron set up a committee to investigate it. They went further than their Barbadian cousins and had the floor of the vault ripped up, hoping, in vain, to find a secret passage. They suspected ghouls, though none of the coffins had in fact been robbed. Forced to give up their fruitless search, the committee laid not sand but ash throughout the vault and chapel and, as at Oistins, left secret seals that would break if the door were opened by any means. For three days and nights the place was guarded by soldiers. Then the committee returned: the seals were unbroken, the ashes were untouched and the coffins were everywhere they shouldn't have been – some standing on their heads, one so badly cracked that a bony arm protruded from it. Lacking the patience of the Barbadians who had put up with this sort of thing for eight years, the Arensburg committee and the Buxhoewdens immediately had the coffins moved elsewhere and put an end to the vault's activities.

What causes coffins to move about, whether they are in vaults in Barbados, in England or on an island in the Baltic Sea? There is no ready explanation. The 'traps' set up by the various investigators – the secret seals and the sand or ash covered floors – strongly indicate that no human villains are involved. That in Barbados it was malevolent Negro slaves – or the malevolent spirits suspected by the Negroes themselves – seems implausible. Among those who have considered the supernatural and paranormal possibilities are Sir Arthur Conan Doyle, who believed that the Oistins coffins moved because of the strange physical powers that are supposed to reside in the bodies of the prematurely dead – like the young Chase girls and Samuel Brewster Ames. There is more credence in the theory proffered by George Hunte, author of *Barbados*, who suggests that 'gas from decomposing bodies and not malevolent spirits was responsible for the violent separations and disarray of the sober arrangements which were made by undertakers'.

What about water in the vaults? Could the coffins have floated? The Chase vault was not only watertight but high and dry too; underground currents can be ruled out. The man who confirmed Mr Paley's letter about the Gretford coffins believed they floated into their strange positions when the vault was

Below: drawings made by eyewitness Nathan Lucas to show how the coffins were originally placed in the vault (left) and how they were found in April 1820 (right). However, there are discrepancies between the account given by Lucas and those of other witnesses, and a second set of drawings (bottom) – also said to have been made on the spot and at the time the tomb was opened – is generally accepted to be a more accurate portrayal of the arrangement of the coffins

Frank Russell compared the drawings in his chapter on the coffin phenomenon in *Great world mysteries* (published in 1957):

As first placed, three large coffins were put in a neat row with the middle one set slightly further away from the vault's door. Three smaller coffins sat tidily on top of the big ones. All had their feet towards the door, their heads towards the back of the vault, their longitudinal axes parallel to the side walls.

When found out of place all coffins were in varying but fairly regular stages of reversal, their heads now being more or less towards the door, their feet more or less towards the back wall. They look exactly as if caught when rotating at snail's pace around their own centres of gravity, some having twisted farther than others, their axes now cutting through an arc of about 120 degrees. The picture they present is that of a swirl, or a spiral effect, like so many metal shapes, heavier at one end than the other, spun around by some force gravitational, gyroscopic, electromagnetic or goodness knows what.

However inconclusive, Russell's suggestion seems the most plausible. Superstition and fear though – slamming the door shut on the case of the creeping coffins of Barbados and abandoning the vault (as at Arensburg) – precluded further scientific research into the whole weird business, which remains wreathed in mystery. All that is known for sure is that for eight macabre years in the Chase vault at Oistins there were, to adapt the words of Emily Brontë, 'unquiet slumbers for the sleepers in that quiet earth'.

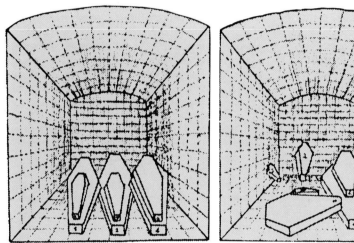
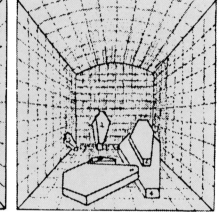

flooded – but there is no evidence that it ever was. Since the events at Arensburg all took place within a few weeks, any sign of flooding would have been noticed; none was. Lead coffins *can* float – they need something to float on, however.

The movements of the Oistins coffins could be ascribed to earth tremors. Barbados lies on a seismic belt and is framed by fracture zones; moreover there is a volcano on the nearby island of St Vincent. The slightest underground tremor could have displaced the coffins – but why only those in the Chase vault? The theory is dubious. Stanton, Gretford and Arensburg are not known for seismic activity.

Most of the coffins in the vault at Barbados were made of lead, so ordinary magnetic forces did not cause the mischief. And yet some such force may provide the answer to the mystery. One vital clue has emerged from the investigations of the Barbadians. At the time of the last burial there in 1819 someone saw fit to make a drawing of the vault in a state of orderliness; and another of its supposedly chaotic appearance when it was opened for the final time in April 1820. Eric

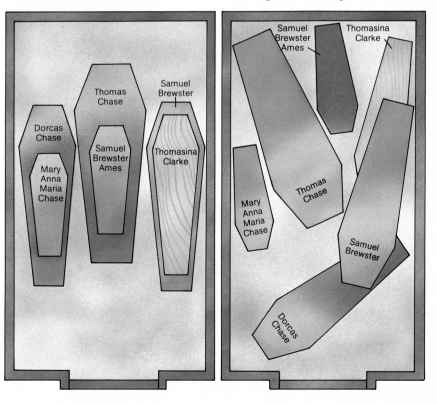

Stalking the Surrey puma

Surrey is one of the most English of counties, a patchwork of commuter towns and rich, rolling countryside. Yet in the 1960s, as CHRIS HALL recounts, a wild, American 'big cat' frightened people and attacked farm animals there

ERNEST JELLETT WILL NEVER forget one Monday morning in 1962. His work for the Mid Wessex Water Board took him to inspect Heathy Park Reservoir, in the North Downs near Farnham, Surrey, early on the morning of 16 July. It is reached by a long track through dense woodland. As a countryman, Mr Jellett is very familiar with the local wildlife – so it was not the rabbit beside the track that surprised him but the big cat-like animal stalking it.

Before he had had time to take this in, things began to happen rather quickly. The rabbit sensed him and fled towards the 'cat', which pounced but missed. Both animals ran up the track towards Mr Jellett. The rabbit made off into the undergrowth, but the other animal bounded straight at him. Having no weapon, he shouted loudly, and fortunately frightened it off.

He later described what he had seen as sandy coloured and resembling a small lion. 'It had a sort of round, flat face, like a big cat, and its tail was long and thin, not bushy. It had big paws.' He was sure it was not a fox.

Later, police searched the area, but found only flattened bracken where 'a good sized animal' had rested. A few days later cattle on a nearby farm were unusually restless,

Bottom: did the lush woods and farmland of Surrey conceal a mysterious big cat during the 1960s? Something resembling a puma (inset) was often seen – but never caught – and such an animal could easily have adapted to the local climate and terrain

Below: Mr A. Burningham, who saw 'an enormous great cat' in late August 1959 while driving past Godsfield Copse, south of Preston Candover. The creature had a cat-like head, mangy looking coat, pointed ears and a tail that curled up – and was, perhaps, a puma

milling about in their field until midnight, as if something unfamiliar were about. Then a woman walking near the village of Crondall saw an animal in a field that she later – having consulted a wildlife book – thought might be a jaguarundi, a South American member of the cat family.

And so began a legend that, after infrequent and isolated reports over the next two years, was to grow to a scale comparable with the Loch Ness monster: the legend of the Surrey puma.

The first account of a strange cat-like animal in Surrey seems to be that recorded by William Cobbett in his *Rural rides*. He recalled seeing it in a tree near Waverley Abbey in his childhood, which would date it around 1770. However, the description he gives could be of a wild cat; these were known in Surrey until at least the 1920s.

New research has revealed several reports from the 1950s that may be related to the puma saga. The most detailed of these occurred at harvest time in 1959, near Preston Candover, 5 miles (8 kilometres) north-east of Winchester.

Another local man, Mr A. Burningham, was driving along a country road in the early evening when 'an enormous great cat' crossed the lane about 40 yards (40 metres) ahead of him. It was the size of a labrador dog, but its head and walk were distinctly feline. He stopped his car and saw the animal, screened by trees, watching lambs in a field, but did not think it wise to leave his

car for a closer look. He was unable to make anything of what he had seen until he noticed the report of Mr Jellett's experience in a local newspaper.

But it was in 1964 that things really began to happen. During the summer, strange cat-like animals were seen around Farnham and near Bordon. A frightful howling kept people awake, likened by one to 'the sound of a hundred cats being murdered.' Then, almost simultaneously, two events brought the mystery to the nation's attention.

Farmer Edward Blanks was manager of Bushylease Farm in Crondall, near Farnham. For two years he had been seeing and hearing a strange cat-like creature that all his countryman's knowledge could not identify. Then in August 1964, a herd of cattle broke out of their field – which they would not have done unless alarmed. One of them was later found bitten and mauled in nearby woods. A vet who examined it was of the opinion that the injuries were not caused by 'any animal found in this country' – though not everyone agreed, and some tried to play down the whole affair.

All the same, by the end of August the hunt was on for the 'Crondall cougar', with Bushylease Farm as hunt headquarters and armed farmers patrolling the woods. They were joined by Billy Davidson, a Canadian ranger with experience of puma tracking who was on holiday in Britain. He did not catch the Surrey puma, but he did find 'definite evidence' of a big cat, including a lair.

In early September there were so many sightings that a mass break-out from a zoo seemed the most likely explanation. A puma was seen at Crondall, and on Farnham Common, and the howling continued. The next

Above: Mr Edward Blanks and his son (left) with a steer apparently mauled by the puma in August 1964. Mr Blanks says the puma was in the area for six or seven years between 1962 and 1969, returning to his farm during March each year. The family got used to it, though it had 'an awful stench'. The big cat seems to have been little trouble, killing only what it needed to survive – and the steer soon recovered

sighting was made by George Wisdom, who had decided to spend his lunch hour gathering blackberries on Munstead Heath, near Godalming. He did not pick many. Whatever it was that snarled at him from the bushes had no wish for his company.

He gave one of the best descriptions of a puma of the whole affair, which is interesting because at this point puma descriptions had not been publicised. Three days later a half-mile (800-metre) trail of footprints appeared overnight in freshly raked sand used for practice gallops by nearby riding stables. Each was 6 inches (15 centimetres) across, and they were identified as possible puma prints by experts at London Zoo.

The many footprints that have been found after sightings of the 'puma' would seem to

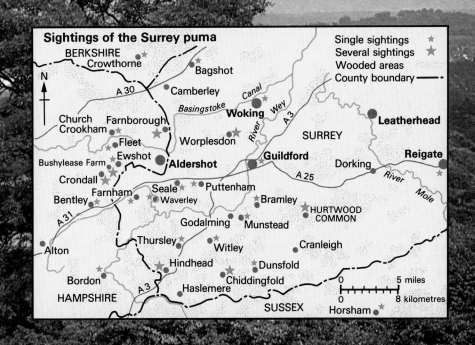

Sightings of the Surrey puma

offer the best hope of evidence for positive identification of the creature. But in fact most of them turn out to have been made by dogs or foxes, and others are too indistinct to be of any help at all. Only two were pronounced puma by the experts: a single print from Hurtwood Common – and the Munstead trail.

Most experts agreed the Munstead prints were of a large cat, probably puma. But naturalist Dr Maurice Burton, who lived nearby and was closely involved in (and sceptical of) the puma affair, found that large dogs could leave similar prints in some circumstances. A St Bernard was missing in the area on the night the footprints appeared, and bloodhounds were kept near the stables.

It is true that some people have claimed that the Munstead print looks more like that of a bloodhound than a puma; but if it was a dog that snarled at Mr Wisdom from the blackberry bushes, it was a very strange dog indeed. He visited a zoo shortly afterwards, and found an identical 'dog' on show. It was in an enclosure marked 'puma'.

After Mr Wisdom's spectacular sighting, the puma became weekly news. A special cage was kept at Godalming police station where an emergency plan to capture the beast, called the 'Munstead monster', was prepared. The public were asked to notify the police promptly, and local papers kept everyone informed. Zoo and RSPCA experts were at hand.

A log of all reports investigated, including unusual attacks on farm animals, was kept by police. When it was finally closed in 1968, it had 362 entries, but there were many more that were either not reported, or that the police for various reasons were unable to investigate.

On safari in Surrey

The most determined efforts to catch the puma took place in 1966, and quite a few serious and not-so-serious 'safaris' were made into the wilds of Surrey in the mid 1960s. These projects ranged from teams of experienced big-game hunters to a local pub selling 'game permits' to would-be puma hunters, with proceeds being donated to charity. But all, whether naturalists or youth clubs, had one thing in common: they failed to find their quarry.

Then, in 1968, it all ended. To this day local lore says that the puma was shot by a farmer, but there is no agreement on where, what became of the body, or why the event received no publicity at the time.

Whatever the truth, the legend lives on, still widely remembered; people still believe they saw the puma. And from time to time its ghost still walks: a few big cats are reported every year in south-east England – for instance, one near Guildford in September 1980, and another at Hastings in December of the same year.

So much at least is legend, but could there

Mr George Wisdom was picking blackberries from these bushes one day in September 1964 when something large and feline snarled at him from amid the foliage. Three days later strange animal footprints appeared nearby – one of only two sets pronounced by experts to be authentic puma tracks

Below: police took this plaster cast of 'puma' footprints from tracks at Bramley Golf Club in 1969

really have been a puma in Surrey? And could it have survived to the present day? Well, it might be improbable, but is not impossible. The climate is milder than much of the puma's natural American habitat. There is no shortage of food: a puma could live on the equivalent of 10 rabbits a day, and the region has tens of thousands of them. Surrey is England's most wooded county; its heaths can be very lonely places where a largely nocturnal animal could roam for weeks unseen.

But where might the puma have come from? In 1964 there were officially just 23 pumas in Britain, all securely behind bars. If it existed, the Surrey puma must have been imported illegally; then it either escaped, or was deliberately freed. If this is correct, it was probably smuggled in as a cub, possibly around 1958.

To support this theory four early sightings were of small big cats, described as 'young puma' in August 1959, 'small lion' and 'jaguarundi' in July 1962, and 'lynx' in January 1963 – but we are left with a 'huge lion' near Fleet in 1959. At a puma exhibition at the Guildford Show in 1966, a young boy was overheard to say he knew a family who had released three puma cubs. Perhaps inevitably he vanished, leaving his story unconfirmed. If it was not a hoax, it would explain everything – but as such proof is lacking, our enquiry must depend on more controversial evidence.

The puma, also known as the cougar or mountain lion, is a shy, mainly nocturnal animal, native to the Americas. It is very adaptable to terrain, being at home in forest or mountains. A full-grown puma would be about 5 feet (1.5 metres) long and 3 feet (0.9 metres) high. Its colour is normally sandy to ginger.

There is no shortage of its alleged sightings, but comparison of their details with the descriptions of a puma is not very encouraging. A shy nocturnal animal should not be seen so often in or near towns in broad daylight. The reported animals are usually too small. Only in colour do we find reasonable agreement, but a number of the creatures are described as black. Black pumas are very rare, and to accept these reports is to accept a double improbability: that there are two pumas in Surrey, one of them a rare type – or that there are both a puma and a panther.

Yet a lot people saw something that they could not identify. Unfortunately, many of the vague descriptions could just as well fit domestic cats or dogs, foxes or deer. Some sightings are very definitely *not* puma.

Others are at considerable distance, very brief, or brief and at night. A significant number are by townspeople, who have little need to know the wildlife in the way a farmer does, and usually take little real notice of it until puma stories appear all over the local paper. It is then a small step to glimpsing next door's ginger tom one night and creating another puma report. Sadly, over three-quarters of the reports must be regarded as suspect.

A camera shy cat

Photographs could solve this problem, but there are few in existence. One, said to show the puma in a garden in Farnham in 1966, cannot be traced. Those taken on a misty autumn morning at Reigate in 1977 are indistinct. The photograph taken at Worplesdon in August 1966 by two ex-police photographers looks suspiciously like a large domestic cat, although one zoologist said its size was like that of a female puma.

To find an animal killed in a way typical of big cats would be good supporting evidence. Pumas generally bring their prey to the ground by hurling themselves against it, and then attack the throat and breast. Some writers on the puma mystery have tended to

Though the Surrey puma saga reached its height in the mid 1960s – and the animal itself was reputedly shot in 1968 – large cat-like animals are still seen in the area and unusual tracks still found. Here 17-year-old Gwen Fraser of Farnborough prepares to measure footprints found in her garden in December 1970

Photographs of the Surrey puma are few and far between, and none of those available are satisfactory. This, taken at Worplesdon in 1966, is supposed to be of the big cat but bears a rather stronger rememblance to a small one of the domestic variety

point to *all* the attacks on farm animals in the region at the time as suggesting puma, an approach that draws justified criticism from sceptics. There are 6000 attacks on farmstock each year, mostly the work of dogs. A dog can inflict terrible injuries, even tearing off whole limbs.

In one case a deer found at Cranleigh could have been killed by a puma. A number of other reports checked by Ministry of Agriculture experts involved injuries 'outside the previous experience' of the officers.

But what of the frightful howling? It could have been made by foxes, badgers or even owls. All the recordings made were identified as fox calls: mating vixen can make perhaps the most terrifying sound of all British wildlife. That leaves us with the sounds reported by farmers – who know the sounds of the countryside – that they had not heard anything like before.

So far we have assumed that either there was no puma at all, or that an ordinary flesh-and-blood puma was loose. Other theories have been put forward to explain how an animal that, by all the rules, should not be there was reported so often.

Some people have claimed that UFOs may be in some way responsible; many have been seen over Surrey, some in places where the puma has also been seen, but many more do not tie into the pattern so conveniently. Timeslips, thought-forms and Bermuda triangle-like vortices have all been suggested. Or is the Surrey puma somehow connected with leys? In 1973 a survey of sightings of mystery cats around Bournemouth showed them all to lie close to leys.

It cannot now be conclusively proven that a puma once prowled the Surrey hills. But it does seem very likely that, at least in the mid 1960s, one did, with remarkably little risk to either human life or farm economy. And it will live on, a blend of reality and imagination, in the folklore of our land.

Dufferin: the fatal flaw

A brilliant diplomat saved from death by the intervention of supernatural forces – this spectacular story, in various guises, travelled the world in the late Victorian period. But how do the facts stand up to scrutiny? MELVIN HARRIS investigates

FATE WAS KIND to the first Marquis of Dufferin and Ava: in 1893 he was saved – so his chroniclers tell us – by supernatural intervention from a violent death.

The story begins some 10 years earlier, when Lord Dufferin was enjoying a welcome break from the incessant bustle of diplomatic life. His distinguished career had already included six years as Governor General of Canada, and in 1883 he was completing a report on British government reorganisation in Egypt. A great house near Tullamore in County Offaly, Ireland, seemed to provide an ideal refuge for anyone seeking tranquillity. But one night, this peaceful idyll was shattered by a terrifying apparition.

Lord Dufferin was in bed when he suddenly found himself wide awake, sick with terror. He had been awoken by strange sounds from the grounds outside – terrifying sounds. However, Lord Dufferin was no coward; he climbed out of bed to investigate. Trembling in every limb and heart racing, he went to the French windows and peered out.

He could see the trim lawns, bathed in moonlight. Almost every section was in plain view, except for one spot, where tall trees cast long black shadows. And from these shadows came the sounds that had woken him – heartrending sobs, more animal than human.

Lord Dufferin began to fumble with the window latches – and, as he did so, a man staggered out of the shadows into the moonlight. He was bent double under the weight of a load on his back. At first sight it looked like a long linen-chest – but, as the man came closer, Dufferin suddenly became aware that the chest was, in fact, a coffin.

Lord Dufferin threw open the windows, ran across the lawn and shouted at the man to halt. Until then the man's face had been held down and hidden, but on hearing the shout

Above: Frederick Temple Hamilton-Temple-Blackwood, first Marquis of Dufferin and Ava (1862–1902). Was he, as his chroniclers insist, saved from death in 1893 by the action of some supernatural power?

Left: the Grand Hotel in Paris. Legend has it that, at a diplomatic reception held here in 1893, an elevator cable snapped, killing all the passengers. Lord Dufferin made a narrow escape by refusing to travel in the elevator – and the story goes that he owed his life to a vision he had had 10 years earlier

Right: the French astronomer Camille Flammarion who, told the story of Lord Dufferin's miraculous escape, published it in his *Death and its mystery* – without, however, checking the facts

he lifted his head and turned it towards Lord Dufferin. And the moonlight fell on a face that was unforgettably loathsome – so contorted with hate that Lord Dufferin stopped dead in his tracks. Then, he drew on his reserves of courage, advanced on the man and walked – right through him!

At the same time the man disappeared – coffin and all. And with his disappearance the gloom lifted and the house and grounds became as calm and restful as ever.

Lord Dufferin returned to his bedroom shaken and puzzled. Then, after writing a complete account of the event in his diary, he managed to snatch some sleep.

At breakfast next morning he read out his account and appealed to his host and fellow guests for an explanation. But no one could help. The description of the man matched no one in the area, past or present. There wasn't even a local ghost to blame – and so the event remained an inexplicable mystery.

Over the years, the memory of that night stayed with Lord Dufferin – but it no longer troubled him. He grew to believe that it really might have been nothing more than an extraordinarily vivid nightmare. And that is how things stood for the next 10 years. Then, in 1893, the vision took on a new significance.

At the time, Lord Dufferin was the British Ambassador to France, and was obliged to attend a diplomatic reception at the Grand Hotel in Paris. When he entered the hotel foyer he found it jam-packed with impatient guests, for the elevator was taking ages to get to the reception area on the top floor. Together with his secretary, he joined the queue for the elevator. Eventually he reached the head of the queue; the elevator arrived, its door squealed open and the attendant waved the guests in.

A hideous double

Lord Dufferin turned pale, stood fast and refused to enter. He mumbled an excuse to the officials with him, then stepped backwards, pulling his secretary after him. Nothing would persuade him to use that elevator, for the attendant was, in every feature, the double of that hideous man he had seen 10 years earlier in Ireland.

The other officials ignored the eccentric Englishman. They crowded into the elevator and it began its laborious climb. Lord Dufferin, meanwhile, went hunting for the manager's office. He had to know who the attendant was and where he came from. But, before the Marquis reached the office there came a disaster. The elevator's cable snapped and it plunged down the shaft to destruction. The passengers were killed outright – as was the ghastly attendant.

No one ever came forward to claim or identify the attendant's body. The hotel manager could answer no questions either, for the attendant was a casual worker taken on for the day. A man without documents or records. Lord Dufferin was baffled. But not

even his money and influence could turn up a single fact about the man. The one certainty was that his strange vision at Tullamore had saved Dufferin's life.

That, in its essentials, is the remarkable story of Lord Dufferin's escape. Published accounts often vary in detail, but no one ever questions the basic truth of the tale. On the contrary, it is always asserted that the facts have been fully researched and investigated. One writer, for example, states that 'The evidence is incontrovertible . . . the details of this story have been carefully investigated by the well-known French psychologist de Maratray, who brought them to the attention of the British Society for Psychical Research.' Another writer adds, 'the accident was reported in the Press . . . but neither the management of the hotel, nor the accident investigators could find any record of the man's name or background.' So, here we seem to have a case that cannot be challenged.

But in fact, the facts are not as watertight as they seem. To begin with, the case was never investigated by the Society for Psychical Research. The society was certainly in existence at the time of the alleged event, but its files prove that it had no record of the Dufferin case. And no newspaper carried reports of the accident – for very good reasons. In fact, the first written account of the Dufferin case did not emerge until 1920 – that is, 18 years after the death of Lord Dufferin and 26 years after the alleged elevator crash.

This primary account was written by the French pyschologist Monsieur R. de Maratray on 18 July 1920. He gave it to the

French astronomer Flammarion, who included it in his book *Death and its mystery*. De Maratray added force to his account by claiming that his wife was related to Lord Dufferin and his family had been kept informed of the events at the time. Flammarion made no attempt to check the story for himself. He even neglected to ask why de Maratray had kept quiet for so long. Instead, he simply took de Maratray's word for everything.

In fact, the fatal accident in the elevator of the Grand Hotel took place in 1878 – some five years before the vision in Ireland, and 15 years before the date of Lord Dufferin's 'miraculous escape'. At the time of that genuine accident there was not a diplomatic reception at the hotel. In any case, Lord Dufferin was not even in Paris – but was serving in Canada as Governor-General. On top of that, in the real accident only one person, a young lady, died – not an elevator full of people, certainly no unknown attendant!

Jettisoning logic

All the facts were established shortly after the publication of Flammarion's book. The intrepid investigator who nailed the story as a lie was Paul Heuze, a journalist with the Paris magazine *L'Opinion*. Heuze proved that, when it came to psychical research, Flammarion jettisoned all the logic and care that went into his astronomical work. As a result his books were crammed full of unsubstantiated stories and hearsay. To his discredit, Flammarion made no attempt to revise these books and the Dufferin story was given wide circulation and picked up by author after author.

But how did such a tale become linked with Lord Dufferin? The files of the Society for Psychical Research provide the answer. They show that in November 1949, a Mr Louis Wolfe of New York wrote to the SPR and asked for details of the society's 'Dufferin investigation'. The SPR replied that it had never been asked to check on the case. But, prompted by this enquiry, the society's secretary then wrote to Lord Dufferin's grand-daughter and asked for her help. In her reply Lady Dufferin stated that the tale did not apply to her grandfather. It was a new version of an old story he used to tell about *someone else*! In the original version, though, an unnamed man had taken his holiday in Scotland, at Glamis Castle. And the vision itself had involved a hearse driven by a man with an ugly and hateful face.

Further research showed that the yarn first appeared as an anonymous second-hand account in the spiritualist paper *Light* of 16 April 1892. *Light*'s editor at the time was the Reverend Stainton Moses and his behaviour paralleled that of Flammarion: he took the tale completely on trust. He wrote this about it: 'It has been communicated to me by a personal friend, and is both authentic and trustworthy.' The account by the Reverend

Moses's personal friend ran as follows: I have just heard from a friend of a remarkable dream. She thought she heard a loud knock on the door, and on looking out she saw that a hearse had stopped at the house. Being greatly surprised, she rushed downstairs and herself opened the hall door. A strange-looking man was on top of the hearse; on seeing her, he said, 'Are you not ready yet?' She said, 'Oh, no; certainly not.' And slammed the door. The sound seemed to have caused her to wake.

She was much puzzled to know what could be the significance of such a very unusual dream. The face of the man haunted her, and for weeks she could not get the remembrance out of her head. All her family and friends were told about the dream, and all the circumstances of it had been discussed.

Some weeks had passed when one day the young lady happened to be in a

Top: Lady Dufferin, grand-daughter of the first Marquis, pictured in 1958. It was she who finally cleared up the origin of the escape story: it was a version of a tale her grandfather used to tell about someone else – a man who had taken his holiday at Glamis Castle in Scotland (above). In Lord Dufferin's original version, however, the apparition had been of a man driving a hearse

large warehouse in the City, and was just going to step into the elevator, when she looked at the man who had charge of it, and immediately drew back, having recognised the face of the man she had seen in her dream. When she drew back her consternation was added to by the exclamation from the man of the very words she had heard in her dream, 'What are you not ready yet, Miss?' Her determination not to ascend in the elevator was confirmed, and she declined to go into it. It only reached to the next floor, when the machinery gave way, the elevator being smashed to pieces and the man killed.

The elevator tale travelled to the United States and Europe, being constantly altered

The face of death

The weird blend of fact and fantasy that characterises the Dufferin tale reached another level of confusion with the release of the classic Ealing movie *Dead of night* in 1945. It was based on a short story by E.F. Benson, *The room in the tower* – itself based on a hearsay version of the Dufferin legend.

The film concerns a group of people at a party, each of whom tells a story about a mysterious happening – and one of the stories is strangely similar to the Dufferin tale. A racing driver dreams, not of a man carrying a coffin, but of the driver of a hearse. And later, the racing driver refuses to get into a bus when he recognises its conductor as the driver of the hearse. The bus subsequently plunges over an embankment.

and added to in its passage. Nine years later, it returned to England in a new guise, now posing as an authentic American event! Ironically enough, it was promptly picked up and reprinted in the pages of *Light*. It seems the new editor and his staff had completely forgotten their earlier account furnished by a 'personal friend' of the Rev. Moses. And on 9 February 1907, it ran the following story under the heading 'Saved by a vision':

The Progressive Thinker gives an instance of a warning dream, as related by Miss Gray, 'A young woman prominent in educational work' in Washington State. While staying in Chicago, where she had planned to visit 'a new department store which had just been opened, whose elevators were death-traps,' she woke up in the middle of the night and saw an unknown face at the window, twenty feet [6 metres] above the ground. On going to the window she saw a hearse standing in the street below, with her nocturnal visitant occupying the driver's box; he looked her squarely in the face and beckoned to her. The next day she visited the store, and on going to one of the crowded elevators the man in charge beckoned to her and said that there was room for one more. His features were those of the man on the hearse in her dream or vision of the night before. She refused to enter the elevator, which 'started down, stuck, and dropped four storeys, killing two of its passengers and injuring everyone else in the car'.

In the meantime, another variation of the story had been incorporated in Lord Dufferin's bag of after-dinner yarns. One day he related it to a young impressionable nephew and gave it special treatment. Adult wiles were not fully appreciated. The twinkle

in Dufferin's eyes was missed. And when he spun out the tale as his very own real-life adventure, the boy was awe-struck and convinced. The boy grew up to become a distinguished diplomat and writer. Out of conviction he retold this 'true story' frequently to his friends – once, unfortunately, to the de Maratrays, who proved as gullible as he himself had been. The innocent culprit, the unwitting father of this tenacious myth was none other than Harold Nicolson.

Right: Harold Nicolson, diplomat and writer – and nephew of Lord Dufferin. Lord Dufferin told the schoolboy Nicolson of his 'escape' – and Nicolson believed it. In adult life he used often to retell the story, so beginning the extraordinarily tenacious myth that, in various guises, was soon known all over the world

Riddle of Racetrack Playa

The stones move – and no one sees them do it. Yet thousands have seen their tracks in the dry lake beds that dot the Sierra Nevada mountains in the western United States. BOB RICKARD tells how the moving stones make their mysterious journeys

HIGH IN THE Sierra Nevada mountains, in the remote region of California's border with Nevada, there are places where stones move at night. Once, a band of pioneers was trapped in these rough, deeply channelled hills and unexpected dried-up lake beds, on their way to prospect or to settle in more hospitable places. Now it is part of the vast Death Valley National Park, of which the moving stones are a great attraction.

Perhaps the most famous of these dry lake beds, or playas, is Racetrack Playa, about $1\frac{1}{4}$ miles (2 kilometres) wide by 3 miles (5 kilometres) long and nearly 4000 feet (1200 metres) above sea level. The visitor's eye is immediately drawn to the scattered boulders and stones that litter this plain of hard, cracked mud. The quality of light at this altitude adds to the surreal effect, so that the rocks, with their snaking furrows behind them, give the impression of being both stationary and stirring. No one has ever seen the stones move – but move they do.

Over the years it was noticed that the rocks that moved had not rolled along but were pushed, leaving a groove the same size as their width behind them. Then in 1955 a geologist called George M. Stanley wrote in the *Bulletin* of the Geological Society of America (GSA) that he believed wind and ice were involved. Stanley was intrigued by the fact that groups of rocks often moved together. He suggested that sheets of ice formed around a group of rocks and that the wind raised the whole sheet slightly and propelled it along. This sounds plausible and was accepted for many years, especially after ice sheets embedded with rocks had been seen moving on other Californian playas. However, the ice layers on the Death Valley playas are extremely thin, and while they may be capable of moving smaller stones, even Stanley did not suggest they could shift the 300- to 600-pound (135- to 270-kilogram) boulders that had made tracks.

The mystery of Racetrack Playa became world-famous in the 1960s, and in 1969 it attracted the attention of Dr Robert P. Sharp, of the California Institute of Technology's geology department, who began a study of the moving stones that lasted seven years. He selected 25 stones of a variety of shapes and weights, up to about 1000 pounds (455 kilograms), named them, and used a metal stake to mark their position. Later he included five more rocks. When he was able to make the arduous journey to the playa over more than 30 miles (50 kilometres)

Opposite: the trail of a moving stone is marked by clear tracks behind it in the arid landscape of Racetrack Playa – one of the dried-up lakes of the Sierra Nevada mountains. The moving stones are a tourist attraction of the Death Valley National Park

These two sets of tracks show how far some of the moving stones travel (right) and how they can change direction (below)

the rock by its movement. This indicated that the rocks must have moved when the playa surface was soft, not during its hard-baked or frozen state. Sharp found that most of the recorded movements occurred in three periods: the particularly wet or stormy winters of 1968 to 1969, 1972 to 1973 and 1973 to 1974. Although only some of the stones moved during all three periods, Sharp could infer that rain was as important a factor as wind. The playas get very little rain – about 0 to 3 inches (0 to 8 centimetres) annually – but they are surrounded by about 70 square miles (180 square kilometres) of hills, which make a fine catchment area. Even a light rain in the area could result in a thin layer of water over most of the playa.

Because the surface of the playa is made of fine clay, the action of the rain creates a sheet of water with clay particles in suspension. If the water soaks the surface deeply enough or for long enough, the rocks get bogged down in soft, sticky clay. But when about a quarter of an inch (0.6 centimetres) of water collects, the surface is firm enough to support the rocks. 'The secret,' Sharp wrote in the GSA *Bulletin* in 1976, 'is to catch the play of wind and water at precisely the right moment.' He thinks that movement probably occurs within one to three days of wet or stormy weather when the surface is 'as slick as a whistle'. A powerful gust of wind is all that is needed to make the rock slide, and a slighter wind afterwards will keep it going. Sharp maintains that the surrounding hills scoop

of rough dirt road, he looked for any tagged rocks that had moved, staked their new position and measured the distance travelled.

During the seven-year study period, 28 of the 30 rocks moved. The longest track measured 860 feet (262 metres) but, as in all cases, this distance was reached by a number of smaller moves rather than all at once. The longest single movement was 659 feet (201 metres) by a 9-ounce (250-gram) cobble called Nancy. The direction of these movements was north-north-easterly, with a few deviations to the east and south-east, which matched the direction of the prevailing winds in the playa.

Sharp soon noticed that there was a ridge on the edges of the furrow and that a small heap of debris was pushed up at the front of

and channel the winds into the playa at sufficient speeds to start the rocks moving – and the smoother the bottom of a stone, the farther it will skid. He has also calculated the maximum velocity of a moving stone as about 3 feet (1 metre) per second.

The phenomenon of moving rocks is not unique to Racetrack Playa. Tracks have been observed on at least 10 other playas in California and Nevada, and from time to time, in the literature of geology, similar anomalies have been reported. In an article written in 1879 for the periodical *Nineteenth Century*, Lord Dunraven told of a strange sight on the shore of a lake in Nova Scotia the previous year:

> One day my Indian told me that in a lake close by all the rocks were moving out of the water, a circumstance I thought not a little strange. However, I went to look at the unheard of spectacle and, sure enough, there were the rocks apparently all moving out of the water on to dry land. The lake is of considerable extent, but shallow and full of great masses of rock. Many of these masses appear to have travelled right out of the lake and are now high and dry some 15 yards [14 metres] above the margin of the water. You may see them of all sizes, from blocks of, say, 6 or 8 feet [1.8 or 2.4 metres] in diameter, down to stones which a man could lift. Moreover, you find them in various stages of progress, some 100 yards [90 metres] or more from the shore and apparently just beginning to move; others halfway to their destination; and others again. . . high and dry above the water. In all cases there is a distinct groove or furrow, which the rock has clearly plowed for itself.

One of the 'walled lakes' in the state of Iowa, USA. According to Professor Charles A. White in a *Scientific American* article (1884), these walls were formed by deposits of compacted gravel, earth and boulders through the action of ice expansion in the shallow lakes. An early theory about the moving stones of the playas maintained that ice formation had caused their movement

Lord Dunraven noticed one enormous specimen some distance from the water's edge; earth and stones were heaped up in front of it to over 3 feet (1 metre) in height. A furrow the exact width of the rock extended down the shore and into the water until it was lost from sight in the depths.

This weird scene, remarkably similar to that on the playas, was explained in a letter to the *Scientific American* later in 1879. The writer, who signed the letter 'J.W.A.', claimed to have seen identical effects in other Canadian lakes. The effect is most prominent in shallow lakes that are partly bounded by steep banks or cliffs, according to the explanation. As ice forms it expands and pushes outwards in all directions. The cliffs form an immovable obstacle on one shore, however, doubling the thrust on the opposite, open shore. In shallow water the ice extends to the lake bottom and embeds the rocks there. As the ice expands, it takes the rocks and any other debris with it, depositing them farther along when expansion stops and a thaw sets in. As the lake ice expands and melts each winter, cumulative movements would be enough to drive the rocks onto the land. A similar explanation was proposed by Professor Charles A. White (*Scientific American* 1884) to account for the mystery of the so-called 'walled lakes' of Iowa, which were originally thought to be 'the work of an extinct race'. He said that successive expansions of ice in shallow prairie lakes gradually deposited substantial ridges of compacted earth, gravel and boulders around the perimeter of the lakes.

So we may know how the rocks move. But the surrealistic scene of playas, rocks and their snaking track marks can still awaken a keen appreciation of the wonder and mystery of the natural world.

The rise and fall of the rope trick

The one conjuring trick that has fired the imagination for centuries – and caused endless speculation – is the Indian rope trick. Is it, as some claim, just a myth? Or an hypnotic illusion? And why is it no longer staged? MARC CRAMER explains how the trick might have been performed

FOR CENTURIES EUROPEAN travellers in India have brought back tales of incredible conjuring tricks of Hindu street magicians, but one trick in particular has seized the imagination: the famous Indian rope trick. Many rumours have grown up around it, including the assertion that it is mere myth, and that one could never find anyone who had seen it themselves, but only heard about it at second, or even third, hand. One thing is sure: the Indian rope trick has prompted more heated debate than any other single conjuring trick. So did it ever happen? If so, how?

Perhaps the answer lies partly in the training of those who performed the trick. Many Indian magicians (or *fakirs*, an Arabic

The conjurer 'Karachi' – an Englishman called Arthur Claud Derby – practises his version of the rope trick in Sussex in 1935. The dummy head on the mat is known as a 'vent head' among stage magicians

word meaning 'the humble ones') are quite capable of achieving genuinely remarkable feats, such as controlling their nervous systems at will, a faculty due to their Yogic training. But fakirs tend also to be excellent showmen with a gift for creating illusions and performing conjuring tricks. Much of their repertoire has been dismissed by Westerners as 'mass hallucination' or 'mass hypnosis', and the legendary rope trick seems obviously to belong to this rather arbitrary category. And it is likely to remain there in popular imagination for there is said to be no one left who knows the real trick and no one living who remembers seeing it performed. Doomed to extinction, the Indian rope trick will be remembered – if at all – as a mass delusion or merely a highly colourful myth.

It is neither. But one may be forgiven for thinking it a myth for it has a long and sensational history. It is unlikely that the West would have heard of the rope trick, let

slight kick and there was the child, who got up and stood quite straight, completely whole.

Since there is no rational explanation for such outrageous deeds as levitating ropes and miraculous resurrections, succeeding generations looked upon Ibn Batutah's report and subsequent accounts as tall tales or blatant chicanery to extract a few coins from the purses of the credulous. It is small wonder that medieval scholars dismissed the rope trick as a complete tissue of lies, and that the Victorians sought to explain it in terms of the new, fashionable science of hypnosis. During the 1890s the British public enjoyed a flirtation with all things psychical and mysterious. Laymen and scientists soon began to argue over the rope trick, often quite bitterly.

The enterprising American newspaper, the *Chicago Daily Tribune*, suffering at the time from a decline in sales, threw its hat into the ring of debate by sending one S. Ellmore, a writer, and a painter called Lessing to distant India with a bold mission to fulfil. They were to photograph, sketch, and ultimately disprove, the infamous Hindu hoax.

Although it was common knowledge that the Indian rope trick was seldom performed, the two Americans soon managed to return

alone taken it seriously, if it were not for the writings of a respected Moroccan explorer and geographer named Ibn Batutah. One evening in the year 1360 he dined with Akbah Khan and a number of honoured guests at the Royal Court in Hang-Tcheou in China. After an enormous meal, the Khan invited his sated guests to join him in the palace gardens where he had arranged a special surprise entertainment. Ibn Batutah noted in his journal that:

When the feast was over, one of the entertainers took a ball of wood in which there were several holes. Through these he passed a rope. He threw it into the air and it went up to a point where we could no longer see it, finally to be held there without visible support. When there was only a little end of the rope in his hand, the entertainer told one of his assistants to hang on to the rope and climb into the air, which he did, until we could no longer see him. The entertainer called him three times with no response. Then he took his knife in hand, as if he were angry, grabbed the cord and disappeared also.

Next, the magician threw on the ground the hand of the child who had climbed the rope, then a foot, after that the other hand, then the other foot, the body and (finally) the head. He came down out of breath, his clothes tinged with blood . . . the entertainer took the limbs of the young boy and put them on the ground in their original position. He then gave the mutilated body a

Far left: this photograph, said to be of the famous rope trick, was taken by an anonymous English soldier in India. It seems, however, that this was merely one of the many rope 'suspension tricks' common in the East

Left: the apparently instant growth of a mango tree. The seed was planted, watered, and covered with a cloth, while the conjurer and his assistants performed their professional patter. The plant was uncovered from time to time, revealing it steadily sprouting – and finally bearing fruit. A clever mixture of sleight of hand and suggestion, this act once rivalled the rope trick in travellers' tales

Below left: an engraving showing a Chinese suspension trick in which performers climbed up ropes, fell down apparently dismembered, and were reassembled by 'magic'

Right: the secret of the classic rope trick:
1 At dusk, the audience are seated around a circle of lanterns, half blinded by the light. Meanwhile the rope has been thrown into the air and invisibly hooked onto a wire out of sight of the spectators. A hidden confederate hoists another, stabilising, wire over the main one.
2 A small, lithe boy begins to climb the erect rope – and disappears.
3 When he insolently refuses to come down, the fakir, apparently seething with rage, climbs the rope himself, with a dagger clenched in his teeth. Then suddenly the horrified audience see the boy's limbs drop one by one to the ground.
4 The fakir then descends the rope, while his assistants stand lamenting around the boy's remains. In fact, the 'limbs' are those of a monkey – and the boy has also descended the rope with the fakir, strapped inside his robes. A few magic words and the boy is whole again

to Chicago with several sketches and photographs that, it seemed, put the death blow to the trick by 'proving' that it was, as suspected, a grand 'mass hallucination'. When their film was developed, the photograph showed only a baggy-trousered Hindu surrounded by an apparently hypnotised crowd. There was no sign of an erect rope, let alone a boy clinging to its top. It was therefore concluded that it was all caused by collective suggestion. The article was printed in August 1890 and it was clear that yet another triumphant debunking had been achieved by the *Tribune*'s sagacious journalists.

A few months passed and another 'daring trick' came to light, but this time one that the *Tribune* had not bargained for. The Lessing-Ellmore illustrations were exposed for the outright fakes they were. Lessing had never set foot on Asian soil and had certainly never witnessed the much-maligned Indian rope trick. What was worse, journalist 'S. Ellmore' *did not exist*. Under pressure, the newspaper's publisher was forced to print a retraction, confessing the elaborate hoax, the object of which was to increase sales.

Thirty years on, the rope trick became news again as a certain Colonel Elliot addressed the London Magic Circle in an

attempt to settle the matter once and for all. In March 1919 the Colonel put up a prize of £500 to anyone who could perform the trick under carefully controlled scientific conditions. Because of the marked absence of London-based fakirs, an advertisement was placed in the *Times of India* offering the fabulous prize to any rope-climbing Hindu able to perform the elusive feat. But the worthy challenge went unanswered.

Much to their frustration, the poor Colonel and his band of eager dilettantes concluded that the trick must therefore be, as rumoured, a myth. It had never occurred to their naïve, ethnocentric minds that fakirs are not the sort of chaps who pass a quiet afternoon at the local gentlemen's club reading English-language newspapers. The fakirs of the 1920s were, for the most part, illiterate even in their own language and could not speak, let alone read, English. The dour gentlemen of the Magic Circle grudgingly agreed with the supporters of parapsychology and came to the tidy conclusion that the Indian rope trick was the product of 'collective hallucination'.

However, some years after the attempts of the Magic Circle to investigate the rope trick, a group of Irish and English soldiers

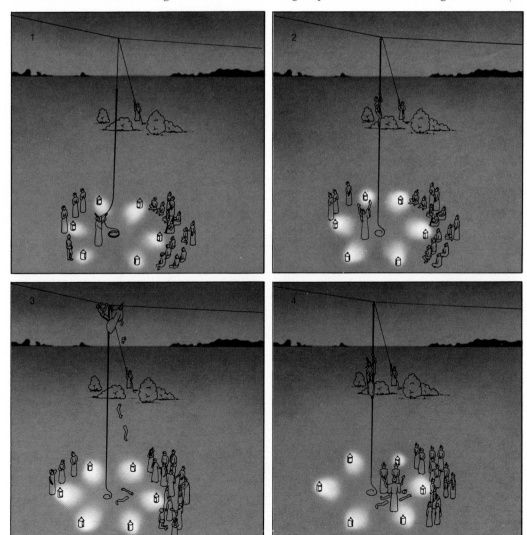

stationed in Upsala, India, witnessed a performance that was almost identical to the feats reported by Ibn Batutah in China in the 14th century – the account of which may be found in the *Journal* of the Society for Psychical Research.

If, for the moment, we imagine the situation reversed and assume that you are a hypnotist touring India and giving demonstrations of your skill to native audiences, it is logical to assume the following. Your audience comprises (say) 50 Hindus from New Delhi (who almost always speak English) and 50 lamas from Sikkim (who rarely ever speak English). Unable to speak either Hindu or Tibetan, you begin to make hypnotic suggestions in English to your audience, and your skills soon take effect. You instruct them to fall into a deep sleep and to 'see' a dragon with gold wings. You are bound to notice that your English-speaking Delhites are busily looking at mythical beasts while there are 50 wide-awake lamas sitting in front of you waiting for something to happen.

The magic of words

The principle seems clear enough. Hypnotic suggestion is, as far as we know, always a verbal procedure and if the subject cannot understand the language of the hypnotist's suggestions, then that person cannot be hypnotised at all.

If mass hypnosis is not the answer, how can we explain the rope trick and the reason why it is so seldom seen?

The secret of the trick has been a closely guarded secret that was handed, like a family heirloom, from father to son. At any given time, the number of people who knew how to perform the trick could be counted on one hand since very few fakirs had the skill or the courage to stage the trick successfully, especially when failure would have inevitably resulted in a broken neck. It is said that by the mid 1940s all the old-time performers

Stills from a film purporting to show the classic rope trick, taken in the 1920s by a European in India. The fakir shows the crowd that the rope is just an ordinary length of hemp (bottom) then throws it into the air where it remains rigid (below). The boy begins to climb up it (below right) and is clearly seen at the top (right). But was this a tame version of the fabled trick or just another clever balancing act?

were far too ancient, or too unsure of their audiences, to bother with the Indian rope trick. But if it was not a myth, how was it actually done?

One might reasonably suspect that the secret is in the rope itself and that joints of metal or bone hold it erect, or that the magician works some sort of hidden device on the ground. But the true secret is literally up in the air.

When the trick was first planned – long before the advent of invisible wires used by today's stage magicians – a long, fine and remarkably strong wire or line was skilfully woven from black hairs. Since this was not completely invisible, the trick was always performed at dusk when the wire would be concealed against a darkening sky. Moreover, it was necessary to perform this version of the trick against a carefully chosen background: never, for example, in a desert or an open space. The only way to avoid

detection was to perform in a valley between two hillocks or knolls. The wire was stretched from one hill to another, spanning the valley so that the fine cord was concealed by the foliage in the background in the same way that modern telephone wires are obscured by a woody countryside but visible against a clear sky. Ever careful to avert the suspicious eye and to win the confidence of his audience, the fakir always began the magic show at dusk and 'warmed up' the crowd with juggling, story-telling and a few banal tricks until the sky was black.

It was at this point that his assistants would come forth with several lanterns and place them at specific points around the seated performer. As this was being done, the magician performed a routine 'patter', deliberately inducing a state of mild boredom and distraction in his audience.

Imagine the scene: as he is chattering to the audience – who are seated some 12 feet

(3.5 metres) in front of him – the fakir removes a length of hemp from a wicker basket and throws it up in the air many times to show that it is just an ordinary rope. Most fakirs will not attempt to slip the wooden ball into the rope in front of their audience but will have concealed it in the rope beforehand. Still chattering, he throws the rope once more into the air. The spectators are now bored, so they fail to notice that on the final handling the magician has slipped a sturdy metal hook into a special hole in the wooden ball. This hook is attached to an extremely fine hair wire, which cannot be seen against the inky sky. The wire leads up to, and over, the main horizontal cord suspended some 60 feet (18 metres) in the air. And as the audience looks up to watch the rope rising into the air by some seemingly magical force they are compelled to stare into the bright lanterns. This creates a partial night-blindness so that the rope appears to be

levitating, reaching up 200 to 300 feet (60 to 90 metres) into the heavens – given that the perspective is cunningly faked. What the audience does not know is that the rope is being hoisted up by a hidden assistant.

From where the audience is sitting it is impossible to see the top of the rope, and when the magician's young assistant refuses his command to climb the rope they can quite see why. The small boy – usually a lad of eight or nine – protests fearfully. Of course, he eventually gives in and climbs up the rope, which begins to sway dramatically. Then suddenly he appears to vanish into thin air. The 'miracle', however is the result of natural camouflage, since the boy is no longer within the range of the lanterns after he has climbed as far as 30 feet (10 metres) or so. When he reaches the top he takes another hook from his dark robes and adds further support to the rope by slipping it in the wooden ball and over the main wire.

Suddenly the fakir shouts out something to the boy, who gives an insolent answer. Apparently seething with anger, the fakir takes up a cruel-looking knife and, placing it between his teeth, he proceeds to climb the rope. In a few moments, he also vanishes. The audience below then hears a bitter argument, followed by screams of mortal agony. And, horribly, one by one the poor lad's limbs fall to the ground with sickening thuds. But these are really only the shaved limbs of a large freshly slaughtered monkey wrapped up in cloth to match the boy's clothing and hidden in the fakir's commodious robes. The conjurer merely removes them and sprinkles them with a little blood he keeps in a glass phial. Finally the boy's severed head – a carefully painted wooden model in a turban – falls to the ground. The audience is in no mood to inspect it.

Four assistants rush to the butchered body, noisily lamenting. Meanwhile, at the top of the rope, the boy slips into a harness inside the fakir's loose clothing, pressing himself against the trickster's stomach while his legs and arms fit into four well-concealed loops. The magician then climbs down the rope with the boy hidden in his robes, and with a noticeably bloodied blade between his teeth. On the ground the magician feigns sorrow as he stares at the hacked-up remains of the lad that are laid out before him. The assistants gather around the grief-stricken fakir and attempt to console him. While this is being staged, the boy slips out of his master's robes and the confederates hide the butchered monkey limbs in their costumes. The assistants' backs form an effective screen that prevents the audience seeing the boy as he lies down on the ground in place of the gory pile. The fakir's confederates step back as the magician utters words of power and gives the little fellow a good, swift kick that – lo and behold! – brings the butchered boy back to life.

A hint of hidden treasure

Since rumours of buried treasure on Oak Island began in 1795, speculators have spent a small fortune trying to find it. EDWARD HORTON describes their attempts – and explains why the treasure remains as elusive as ever

ON A SUMMER'S DAY in 1795 a 16-year-old lad named Daniel McGinnis beached his canoe on the south-eastern shore of a small island in Mahone Bay, which makes a deep indentation in the southern coast of Nova Scotia. Why McGinnis chose this particular island for his excursion is unknown. Perhaps he was attracted by the feature that distinguishes the island from its neighbours – a thick covering of red oak, which had given rise to its unofficial name, Oak Island.

McGinnis set off for the interior of the island, following an old path through the trees. Presently he found himself in a clearing, where the oak trees had been cut down and a second growth was springing up to take their place. Curiously, however, there stood in the centre of the clearing a single, ancient oak. McGinnis noticed that one of its branches had been lopped off and that the stump overhung a depression in the earth from a height of about 15 feet (5 metres). The depression, and the fact that he could plainly see lacerations on the stump, which he took to be scoring from a rope, suggested to McGinnis that he had stumbled upon the site of buried treasure. He hurried back to his home town of Chester, 4 miles (6 kilometres) distant on the eastern shore of Mahone Bay, to enlist the aid of friends.

The following day McGinnis returned to Oak Island, accompanied by 20-year-old John Smith and 13-year-old Anthony Vaughn. With picks and shovels the boys set to work beneath the tree.

No sooner had they begun shovelling out the loose earth than they discovered that they were indeed following in someone's footsteps. For they found themselves in a clearly defined circular shaft, 13 feet in diameter, with walls of hard clay that bore the marks of

As the units of measurement used in early records of excavations at the Money Pit were Imperial, in this article the original measurements have not been converted into metric equivalents. The following conversion chart may be helpful.

1 inch=2.5 centimetres
10 inches=25 centimetres
1 foot=30 centimetres
10 feet=3 metres
100 feet=30 metres
1 mile=1.6 kilometres

Right: this diagram shows the various levels of the Oak Island Money Pit found by successive treasure-seeking expeditions from 1795 to 1850. The ingenious system of tunnels that ensured the flooding of the pit each time it was excavated beyond a certain depth can clearly be seen

Left: Oak Island lies off the coast of Nova Scotia, sheltered by the wide sweep of Mahone Bay. The aerial view (far right) shows how successive excavations have eaten away at the coastline close to the Money Pit, which is situated in the foreground of the photograph, to the right

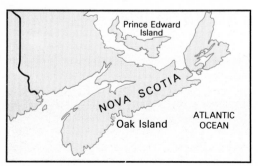

Prince Edward Island

NOVA SCOTIA

Oak Island

ATLANTIC OCEAN

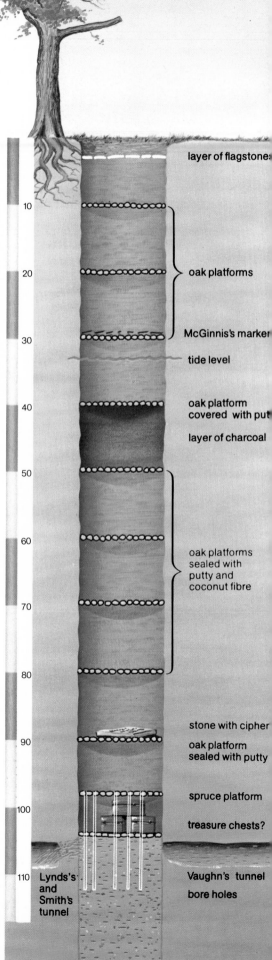

layer of flagstones

oak platforms

McGinnis's marker

tide level

oak platform covered with putty

layer of charcoal

oak platforms sealed with putty and coconut fibre

stone with cipher

oak platform sealed with putty

spruce platform

treasure chests?

Vaughn's tunnel

bore holes

Lynds's and Smith's tunnel

picks. Four feet down they encountered a layer of flagstones, which could not have come from Oak Island. They hauled them out and kept digging. At 10 feet they ran into a platform of solid oak logs extending right across the shaft and firmly embedded in its clay walls. They managed to remove the logs and dug on. At 20 feet there was a similar platform, and at 30 feet yet another. With such limited equipment the lads could go no further – indeed, it was a prodigious feat for them to have got as far as they did. They returned to Chester to drum up more support, having first driven in stakes to indicate the depth they had reached.

Surprisingly, in view of the obvious allure of buried wealth and the intriguing nature of their discovery, the boys found no takers. Apparently Oak Island had a shady reputation. It was haunted – dangerously so. A Chester woman, whose mother had been one of the first settlers in the area, recalled that fires and strange lights had once been observed on the island. A boatload of men had set off to investigate these goings-on and had disappeared without trace. Clearly, the place should be given a wide berth.

It was nine years later, when the boys had grown into men, that help finally came forth in the shape of one Simeon Lynds, a well-heeled 30-year-old who became interested in the story as told him by Vaughn and who formed a syndicate to assist the original three in their quest. John Smith at least had not been idle all this time. He had managed to buy the land surrounding the excavation, and indeed over the next three decades would add to his holding, lot by lot, until he was in possession of the whole eastern end of the island. So it was that in 1804 a group of determined men, well-equipped for the task in hand and confident of success, descended on the mysterious Oak Island.

First they had to clear out the mud that had settled in the pit, but once they came to the sticks left nine years before, they were satisfied that their site had been unmolested during the intervening years. They now set to work in earnest. Reports of what they encountered between 30 feet and 90 feet down vary both in detail and in sequence, but the following account is accurate in its essence and does not sensationalise the discoveries made by the syndicate of 1804. At the 40-foot level they found another oak platform, this time covered in putty; at 50 feet, having dug through charcoal, they came upon yet another oak platform, this one sealed with coconut fibre. Then at regular 10-foot intervals there were more platforms, all of oak, either unadorned or covered with putty or coconut fibre.

Indecipherable inscription

At a depth of 90 feet they hit a flat stone, 3 feet long and 1 foot wide. It was not native stone and, of more significance, it bore an indecipherable inscription on the underside. This stone, with its strange markings, was surely a most valuable clue, but it was apparently treated in an off-hand manner. John Smith installed it at the back of the fireplace in the house he had built on the island, a move that was hardly calculated to preserve any message the stone was intended to convey. Half a century later the stone was exhibited in Halifax, as a lure for the recruitment of further funds for exploring the pit. At that time a professor of languages claimed to have cracked the code: 'Ten feet below two million pounds.' Someone who saw the stone in the early years of this century recalled in 1935 that whatever inscription there was had faded completely by the time he saw it, and his must be the final word – literally; no one has been able to trace the stone since then.

The treasure hunters pressed on, now with a crowbar. The earth was so sodden that they had to haul up one cask of water to every two casks of earth. At 98 feet they struck

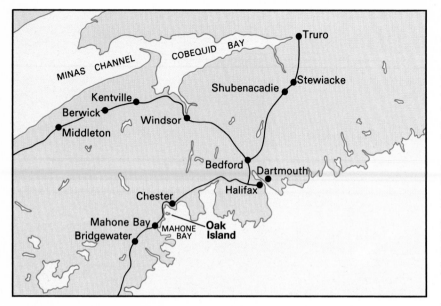

something solid, stretching across the entire width of the shaft. They reckoned that it was wood – and it required only a small leap of faith to conclude that it must be a chest. It was nearly nightfall on Saturday, and the men returned to their homes, confident that Monday morning would bring them riches beyond the dreams of avarice.

In fact, Monday morning brought nothing but disappointment. To their chagrin, they found the pit filled with water to within 33 feet of the surface. They tried to bale it out with buckets, but the level remained stubbornly unchanged. They rigged up a pump and lowered it to the 90-foot level. The pump burst, and the syndicate abandoned work for the year.

In the spring of 1805 they returned to the site and tried to drain the pit by digging another, deeper one alongside. At 110 feet, still dry, they tunnelled sideways towards the original shaft – to be greeted by a veritable Niagara. They were lucky to escape with their lives (as some of their dogged successors did not). By the following morning the débâcle was complete. Having once been only inches from their goal, so they had believed, they now stared glumly at two muddy pits, both filled with water to within 33 feet of the surface. They had exhausted their capital and now admitted defeat, blaming their misfortune on a caprice of nature. They would not be the last to mistake the identity of their unseen adversary.

For 44 years the Money Pit, as it was to become known, lay undisturbed, but then in 1849 a new syndicate was formed, with an ageing Anthony Vaughn acting in an advisory capacity. The Truro syndicate (named after the town in which it was formed) found both shafts caved in, but 12 days' hard labouring took them 86 feet down the original shaft. As had happened half a century before, the diggers left for home on a Saturday evening, light of heart. An inspection on Sunday morning showed nothing

A map of Mahone Bay and Oak Island. It was here that the search for buried treasure began when, one summer's day in 1795, 16-year-old Daniel McGinnis paddled his canoe across Mahone Bay to explore Oak Island – and stumbled on the Money Pit

amiss, and the men set off for church in Chester, doubtless to render heartfelt thanks. If so, their gratitude was premature. When they returned at 2 p.m., 'to their great surprise [they] found water standing in the Pit, to a depth of 60 feet, being on a level with that in the Bay.' Their attempts to bail it out were described in an account a few years later as being 'as unsatisfactory as taking soup with a fork'.

Undismayed, the Truro men decided to employ a pod auger (a horse-driven drill that could bring to the surface samples of what it penetrated) in order to determine precisely what it was that the pit contained below the 98-foot level. They erected a platform above the water and bored five holes, the first of them to the west of centre of the pit, the others progressively eastward across the pit. The first two revealed only mud and stones.

The third, however, was a different matter. In a written report, the man in charge of the drilling operations commented as follows:

The platform was struck at 98 feet just as the old diggers found it, when sounding with the iron bar [in 1804]. After going through the platform, which was 5 inches thick, and proved to be spruce, the auger dropped 12 inches and then went through 4 inches of oak; then it went through 22 inches of metal in pieces; but the auger failed to bring up anything in the nature of treasure, except three links resembling the links of an ancient watch chain. It then went through 8 inches of oak, which was thought to be the bottom of the first box and the top of the next; then 22 inches of metal, the same as before; then 4 inches of oak and 6 inches of spruce, then into clay 7 feet without striking anything.

This was certainly exciting, and the fourth bore was no anticlimax. Eighteen inches below the platform the drill appeared to scrape the side of a chest (so they surmised), and in fact splinters of oak were brought to the surface, along with what they took to be coconut fibre.

Double dealing

The fifth and final bore took a bizarre turn. The foreman, James Pitblado, was under instructions to remove every speck of material clinging to the drill when it was brought to the surface, so that it could be examined under a microscope. This he did, but not quite in the spirit intended. He was seen by one of the syndicate members to take something out of the auger, wash it, study it closely and slip it into his pocket. When challenged, he blithely retorted that he would display his findings at the next meeting of the syndicate directors. Incredibly enough, he was taken at his word. Instead of attending the board meeting, Pitblado found himself a backer, who promptly made an unsuccessful attempt to buy the eastern end of Oak Island. It was commonly believed that what Pitblado found was a jewel.

The Truro syndicate was now convinced to a man – and not without good reason – that two oak chests filled with loot lay, stacked one on top of the other, immediately below the 98-foot level. It remained merely to conquer nature's obstinacy over the matter of the water. In the spring of 1850 a new shaft was sunk some 10 feet to the west of the Money Pit: hard clay to a depth of 109 feet, and no flooding. Then another shaft was bored sideways into the Money Pit, just as in 1805, and with the same result: water burst in, half-filling it within minutes.

It is hard to credit, but it seems that it was only at this stage in the saga that anyone got round to questioning the source of all the water that was so bedevilling things. The story goes that someone tumbled into one of the pits, swallowed a mouthful and pronounced the water *salt*! In any case, it is a fact that only at this juncture was a connection made between the water in the shaft and the sea surrounding Oak Island. The association between the two was easily confirmed by noting that the water in the shafts rose and fell with the tides.

The composition of the soil ruled out any possibility of natural seepage (which would have made it impossible to dig the Money Pit in the first place anyway), so there was only one conceivable explanation. The Money Pit was in some way or other connected with the sea by a subterranean passage. How?

The answer was not difficult to find. A quick search on the nearest beach, 500 feet from the Money Pit at Smith's Cove, revealed all. When the tide ebbed, the sand 'gulched water like a sponge being squeezed'. A bit of spadework showed why. At a depth of 3 feet the workmen turned up a 2-inch layer of the now familiar coconut fibre. Beneath this was a 5-inch layer of kelp, or seaweed, then carefully arranged flat stones, criss-crossing one another. This 'sponge' extended for 145 feet along the beach, between low and high water marks. Next the searchers uncovered five box drains, skilfully constructed of flat stones, 8 inches apart, at a depth of 5 feet. These drains converged, fan-like, on a funnel-shaped sump hole, just above high-water mark. (When one of the drains was uncovered it was completely free of silt – a comment on the high quality of the original workmanship.) From the sump a tunnel ran inland and steadily downwards to the Money Pit, finishing its 500-foot course somewhere below the 98-foot mark.

The present-day observer, like the men from Truro, is driven to accept a remarkable conclusion – a conclusion that, were it not for incontrovertible evidence, he would be inclined to laugh out of court. Someone, at some time prior to 1795, had badly wanted to conceal something. Either by chance or by design, he set about his business on an obscure island in a Nova Scotia bay. He started by digging a shaft to a depth of over 100 feet. Then he constructed a 500-foot tunnel between the shaft and the beach at Smith's Cove, where he constructed a fiendishly clever bit of 'plumbing' that booby-trapped the approach to his hiding place. He then filled in the shaft, having rendered it inaccessible in its lower reaches, not haphazardly but in a most deliberate manner. Finally, having switched on the burglar alarm, as it were, he sailed off into the sunset, leaving behind the tell-tale oak tree.

The men from Truro were awed, as well they might be, but not overawed. What 17th- or 18th-century Man could ravel, 19-century Man could unravel. Or so he thought.

Smith's Cove on Oak Island. Here treasure hunters discovered the secret of why the Pit flooded each time they reached a certain level in their excavations

Over the years scores of prospectors made their way to Oak Island, each one convinced that he would recover the fabulous treasure from the ingenious Money Pit.

IF THE TREASURE SEEKERS of the Truro group had ever wavered in their belief in the existence of a fabulous hoard at the bottom of the Money Pit, the discovery of the ingenious flood tunnel enabled them to cast off any doubts. Quite apart from the sheer brilliance of the tunnel arrangement, the task of building the pit had been nothing short of Herculean. It was inconceivable that someone would go to such lengths to protect run-of-the-mill booty. The Money Pit must harbour a fortune, and it was well worth any amount of effort to reach it.

Accordingly, the workmen built a coffer dam 150 feet long across Smith's Cove, between the low-water mark and the catchment, hoping thereby to cut off the water supply. It would then remain only to pump the Money Pit dry once and for all. Unfortunately, a particularly high tide swept the dam away before it was completed. The Truro men then compounded their misfortune by misjudgement.

It should have been plain to them that it was possible to build a dam successfully, for how, without making one himself, could their mysterious predecessor have dug his tunnel in the first place? Yet instead of persevering with their original plan, they opted for a quicker, cheaper solution. They decided to intercept the tunnel between the shore and the Money Pit and to block it off. The reports are confused about how many fresh shafts they sank, and where, in an attempt to locate the tunnel. At one point they thought they had it, when they dislodged a boulder at a depth of 35 feet and were greeted by a surge of water. In fact, they

As the units of measurement used in early records of excavations at the Money Pit were Imperial, in this article the original measurements have not been converted into metric equivalents. The following conversion chart may be helpful.

1 inch=2.5 centimetres
10 inches=25 centimetres
1 foot=30 centimetres
10 feet=3 metres
100 feet=30 metres
1 mile=1.6 kilometres

Oak Island, which takes its name from the thick growth of red oaks that covers both its ends, seen here from the coast of Nova Scotia. A tiny, uninhabited island, it became a hive of activity after the discovery of the Money Pit in 1795. Through the years men and equipment were taken to the island by boat, but in 1963 Robert Dunfield, an American petroleum geologist, built a causeway from the mainland (this can be seen at the right of the photograph) to facilitate the transportation of heavy machinery

were far too close to the Money Pit for the flood tunnel to be so near the surface, and when they attempted to seal off the supposed tunnel by driving stakes and timbers into it, the water level in the Money Pit remained undisturbed. Thwarted, they resorted to an expedient that had been tried before. Fifty feet from the Money Pit, they dug down to a depth of 118 feet and then tunnelled sideways towards their goal. They were even more unlucky than their predecessors had been: the pit collapsed into the tunnel.

This was worse than anything that had happened before, and the Truro men believed that in the subterranean turmoil their treasure 'chests' had tumbled deeper into the shaft, perhaps to a depth of 150 feet. Whether or not that bleak conclusion was justified, this latest development was more than a minor setback. Where before there had been 'chests' lodged securely around the 100-foot mark, there was now chaos, a dreary sea of mud in which their dreams of wealth lay trapped. Their funds were exhausted, and they called a halt.

In 1859 the group re-formed, and the following year there emerged a new Truro syndicate, which nevertheless numbered some of the original members. More shafts were sunk, all with the purpose of blocking off or diverting the flow of water from the flood tunnel, and all with the same conspicuous lack of success. As many as 33 horses and 63 men were employed at the pumps at one time, and then in 1861 steam power was harnessed to the seemingly insuperable task of draining the Money Pit. The boiler burst, scalding one of the workmen to death. By 1865 the men from Truro had had enough and quit for good, making way for a new syndicate from Halifax, which was formed the following year.

Like the original Truro syndicate, the Halifax group set about things the sensible

Sinking into the quagmire

way. They tried to cut off the water at source by building a dam. As before, the tide demolished their handiwork before it was completed, and, as before, this single failure deflected the treasure seekers from their sound strategy. Instead of buckling down to the arduous business of building a *better* dam, they returned to the Money Pit. They pumped and they dug; they bored holes and dug some more, running branch tunnels laterally in an attempt to intercept the flood tunnel. This they finally accomplished, although it did them no good. They discovered that the flood tunnel, some 4 feet high and 2½ feet wide, entered the Money Pit at a depth of 110 feet (that is, 10 feet below the supposed original location of the treasure). But finding the flood tunnel and cutting off the flow of water from the sea were two different matters, and in 1867 the syndicate gave up the unequal struggle. Before his death in 1938, one of the syndicate members, Isaac Blair, told his nephew Frederick Blair (who would himself be closely involved with many attempts to solve the Oak Island mystery during his long life): 'I saw enough to convince me that there was treasure buried there and enough to convince me that they will never get it.' Prophetic words.

A sound analysis

By now the pattern of failure was pretty clearly defined, and a quarter of a century was to elapse before the next brave attempt. Then in 1894 the Oak Island Treasure Company was established, with $60,000 capital. The young Blair drew up the prospectus, which was certainly sound enough in its historical analysis. Eager investors were told: 'It is perfectly obvious that the great mistake thus far has been in attempting to "bail out" the ocean.' The answer, it suggested, was 'to use the best modern appliances for cutting off the flow of water

Above: the head of the Money Pit at the time of the excavations by Frederick Blair's Oak Island Treasure Company. Over a period of about five years Blair and his associates made repeated attempts to drain the pit – but without success

Below: a group of eager prospectors at work at the Money Pit in about 1915. Blair's own funds had long since run out, but he continued to act as an adviser to other syndicates that arrived on the island. Right up to his death in 1954, Blair remained convinced that the elusive treasure would be found

through the tunnel at some point near the shore, before attempting to pump out the water'.

As so often before, an attempt to intercept the flood tunnel was made close to the Money Pit rather than near the shore (where it must lie nearer the surface), and with the usual inconclusive results. Then, again as before, the Money Pit itself was attacked – with added difficulty now because the century-long depredations had obscured its precise location. Blair and his associates found it, however, by working their way upwards from one of the side tunnels leading off an earlier shaft. (By this time a cross-section of the area would have resembled a rabbit warren.) They discovered the flood tunnel too, where it entered the Money Pit at the 110-foot mark. But the tidal water pressure was far too great to stem at that point.

It was 1897 by the time Blair and his colleagues belatedly turned their attention to the beach at Smith's Cove. They had no intention of building a dam, but they launched a determined assault on the flood tunnel, near its source. They bored five holes in a line running across the supposed path of the flood tunnel, and one of them yielded salt water, which rose and fell with the tides. They lowered 160 pounds (73 kilograms) of dynamite to a depth of 80 feet, and when they set it off, they observed considerable turbulence in the Money Pit. Assuming that they had finally destroyed the flood tunnel, they returned to the Money Pit and the pumps, but still the water poured in.

According to the traditional sequence of events, it was now time to start drilling. First they sank a 3-inch pipe, which came to rest against iron at 126 feet. Inside the pipe they lowered a drill, which went past the obstruction and struck what was identified as cement at 151 feet. Twenty inches further on the drill struck oak 5 inches thick. Then it hit what 'felt like' large metal objects, which persistent twisting and turning of the auger

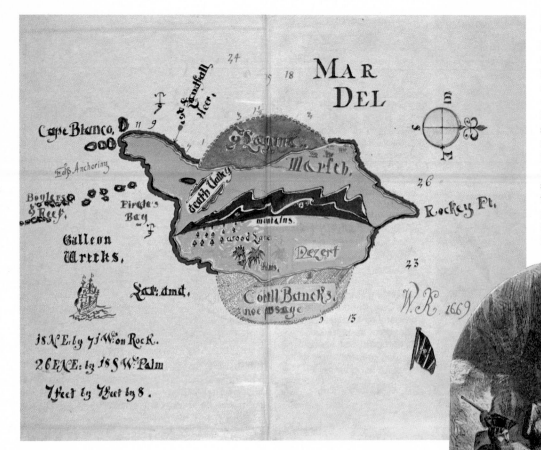

On the chart (as labeled): MAR DEL, Cape Blanco, Galleon Wrecks, Pirate's Bay, Rockey Pt., Dezert, Coull Bancks noe passage, W.R. 1669

is N.E. by 7⅟ W: on Rock.
26 E.N.E: by 18 S W. Palm
7 feet by 7 feet by 8.

So near, yet so far

Who was the engineering genius behind the Money Pit? What did he bury there – and why? After years of investigation all hope of solving the mystery was abandoned. But there was one vital clue that everyone had overlooked

FROM THE MOMENT that Daniel McGinnis chanced upon the Money Pit in 1795 to the present day, attempts to salvage the supposed treasure have naturally gone hand in hand with speculation about the identity of those who buried it. There has been no shortage of candidates, from a tribe of Incas to a party of Norsemen. Dottiest of all, surely, is the theory that the Money Pit conceals manuscripts of Francis Bacon's that reveal his authorship of Shakespeare's plays. All along, however, the popular favourites for the role have been pirates – either pirates unknown or one particularly well-known pirate, Captain William Kidd.

This is hardly surprising, given the romantic association between pirates and buried treasure. And while, generally speaking, the pirate connection has been regarded as self-evident, there is at least one small piece of circumstantial evidence that appears to confirm such a suspicion. The oft-mentioned coconut fibre (if it was correctly identified) presumably came from the West or East Indies, notorious haunts of pirates and buccaneers. Nova Scotia is far from the beaten track of piracy, but there is certainly no reason why some of the English maurauders who preyed so successfully on Spanish ships and towns in the Caribbean during the middle part of the 17th century, the notorious 'brethren of the coast', should not have made their way up the Atlantic coast.

It is an attractive theory that conjures up visions of pieces of eight, a frenzy of moonlit activity by desperate men with the sea at their backs, blood on their hands and avarice in their hearts. But it founders on the question of dates. It will be recalled that McGinnis found a clearing with young oaks springing up to replace those that had been felled. The red oaks of the North American and Canadian coast grow quickly, and McGinnis would have found mature trees towering above him, not saplings, had the Money Pit been dug a century and more before.

The identification of the pirate in question as Captain Kidd presents difficulties too. He

As the units of measurement used in early records of excavations at the Money Pit were Imperial, in this article the original measurements have not been converted into metric equivalents. The following conversion chart may be helpful.

1 inch=2.5 centimetres
10 inches=25 centimetres
1 foot=30 centimetres
10 feet=3 metres
100 feet=30 metres
1 mile=1.6 kilometres

was hanged for piracy at Wapping in 1701 and has subsequently been popularly associated with practically every tale of buried treasure that has ever been told. Nevertheless, Kidd and the mysterious Oak Island brush against each other in a strange way.

In 1935 a book entitled *Captain Kidd and his Skeleton Island* appeared in England. It included a map of an island and a set of directions. The map was based, according to the author of the book, Harold T. Wilkins, on the famous Kidd charts, which had recently come into the hands of a collector of pirate relics, Hubert Palmer. The charts, four of them, had been found hidden in three sea chests and an oak bureau – apparently genuine Kidd relics. All depict an unidentified island in greater or lesser detail, and they contain various markings and inscriptions (not all of them identical, although the island is always the same), including the initials W.K., the location 'China Sea' and the date 1669. These Kidd-Palmer charts, as they are known, were accepted by experts as being genuine 17th-century documents.

There are striking similarities between the island depicted in these charts and Oak Island, despite the 'China Sea' location. It has been suggested, incidentally, that the latter is both a red herring and, rather whimsically, a pun on *la chêne*, French for 'oak'. These similarities almost leaped off the page at Gilbert Hedden, who came across Wilkins's book as he was mounting his campaign on Oak Island in 1937. And Wilkins's drawing, apparently based on the original charts, contained these clear directions:

18 w and by 7 E on Rock
30 SW 14 N Tree
7 by 8 by 4

Hedden set out on a determined exploration of the area around the Money Pit with Wilkins's book open in his hands. Fifty feet

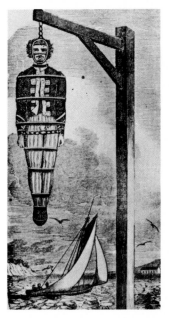

Below: this map, from Harold Wilkins's book *Captain Kidd and his Skeleton Island*, convinced prospector Gilbert Hedden that Skeleton Island was in fact Oak Island, and that there was indeed an immense treasure buried there. But the map came from Wilkins's imagination, and it bears little resemblance to any of the genuine Kidd-Palmer charts

north he came upon a large granite boulder with a hole drilled in it. When he told Isaac Blair of this, the old campaigner was reminded of a similar stone that he and his associates had come across 40 years earlier, down at Smith's Cove. The two men found the stone, similarly drilled, and paced out the distance between the two, which was approximately 140 yards. In an attempt to relate this distance to the information contained in Wilkins's book ('18 w and by 7 E'), they estimated that they had paced 25 rods (1 rod is 16½ feet).

Then two land surveyors were called in, who calculated a position 18 rods from the rock by the Money Pit and 7 rods from the one at Smith's Cove. From that point they measured 30 rods south-west, following the directions in the chart. And there, beneath tangled undergrowth, they found a triangle of beach stones, each side of which was 10 feet long; its base was enclosed in an arc, giving the appearance of a rough sextant. An arrow of stones ran 14 feet from the curved base of the triangle to its apex. The arrow pointed north, straight at the Money Pit. Hedden and Blair could make no sense of the third line of instructions, but they had seen enough to convince them that Captain Kidd's island and Oak Island were undoubtedly one and the same.

A mythical island

So persuaded was Hedden by this discovery that he journeyed to England to discuss it with Wilkins. Wilkins was flabbergasted. He explained that he had drawn the map from memory, that it was a composite of the four Kidd-Palmer charts that Palmer had only allowed him to glimpse, that he had had no chance to make a note of the directions that two of the charts contained. So where had Wilkins got those directions he published with his drawing – directions that had led Hedden to his discovery on Oak Island? The author was adamant: he had simply made them up. When pressed further by Hedden, Wilkins confessed that the *map itself* had come straight from his imagination too – that Palmer had refused his request for a sight of the original charts. As for Oak Island, he had never heard of it, had never seen its outline, had never in fact crossed the Atlantic. Yet he had to concede that his mythical island did indeed look like Oak Island, and that Hedden had proved that those fanciful directions did indeed correspond to something very real. By the time Hedden left England to return to Oak Island, Wilkins appeared to have convinced himself that he was no less than the reincarnation of Captain Kidd.

Hedden went away shaking his head in bewilderment, which is all anyone could do about this aspect of the Oak Island mystery until the answer to the Wilkins enigma was provided by Rupert Furneaux, in his book *Money Pit, the mystery of Oak Island* (1972). Furneaux discovered that Wilkins had lied to

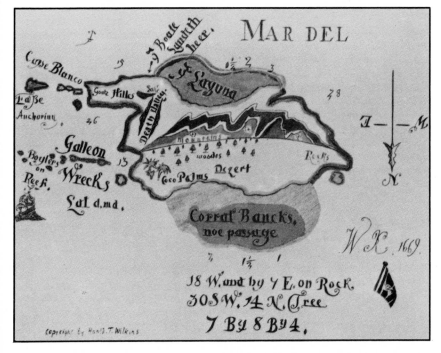

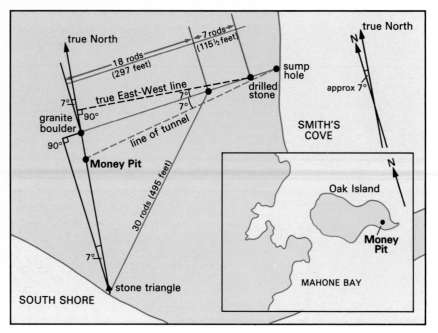

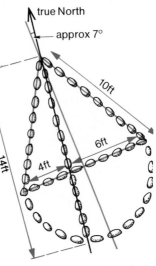

Hedden. Wilkins had in fact been corresponding with a Nova Scotian, who in 1912 had chanced upon a box containing charts among a pile of stones on an island 15 miles (24 kilometres) north of Mahone Bay. Those charts are now lost or hidden, but someone who had seen them was able to draw for Furneaux, from memory, the mystery island depicted in the charts, complete with directions. Moreover, in the charts the island was named Gloucester Isle, which, Furneaux had already discovered, was the name given to Oak Island when Mahone Bay was charted by the British Admiralty hydrographer, Joseph Frederick Wallet Des Barres, in 1773. The Des Barres charts of various parts of the Atlantic coast were not printed until later that decade, by which time the war raging between Britain and the American colonies would certainly have ensured that they were closely guarded documents. Hence, according to Furneaux, the inescapable conclusion is that whoever buried the charts that were discovered in 1912 had access to the Des Barres chart of Mahone Bay and merely added his own directions to mark the location of the Money Pit (*his* Money Pit, it follows). Wilkins had blithely reproduced these directions and the island shaped like Oak Island in his book on Captain Kidd, thereby adding confusion to genuine mystery – the mystery of who buried what on Oak Island. (There is a further mystery: the island in the Kidd-Palmer charts bears an unnerving resemblance to Oak Island; this is inexplicable.)

In his book Furneaux claimed to have worked out a plausible solution to the mystery, and he reasons his case carefully, sifting the known from the speculative, weighing the likely against the improbable. As he sees it, everything points in one direction.

Furneaux ridiculed the commonly held notion that the Money Pit and its elaborate defences were the work of pirates – the

Top: the course plotted by Gilbert Hedden and Frederick Blair (who was still acting as unofficial adviser to operations on Oak Island), following the directions on Harold Wilkins's map. This led to the discovery of a triangle of stones (above) embedded in the soil beneath a dense tangle of undergrowth, and within the triangle was an arrow – pointing directly at the Money Pit

redoubtable Kidd or any of his ilk. First, the idea that pirates went around burying treasure chests is largely a fiction; it runs counter to the 'live for today' mentality of thieves in general and pirates in particular. Crews of pirate ships were paid on a share basis and on the nail, since, like all seamen, they demanded the right to squander their hard-earned money in time-honoured pursuits at the end of the voyage. Why would they help their captain to hide the spoils on some remote island to which they would, in all likelihood, never return?

This argument is mere conjecture, but it makes a great deal of sense. Even more telling is Furneaux's contention that to ascribe to pirate riff-raff a scheme so brilliant in conception and so masterful in execution is simply ludicrous. According to one authority whom Furneaux consulted, the tunnelling operation would have taken 100 disciplined men, working in three shifts, six months to accomplish. Whoever it was who directed them in this back-breaking enterprise, he was a trained engineer of outstanding quality.

Finally, there is the date of construction, which has already been mentioned in connection with the sapling oaks. If Furneaux was right that whoever did the job must have access to the Des Barres chart (which means that the work was undertaken some time after the mid 1770s), then pirates are ruled out virtually on that score alone, since their halcyon days in the Caribbean and along the Atlantic coast were long gone by that time.

A most important clue

So, if pirates were not responsible for the Money Pit, then who did built it? And how? And why? According to Furneaux, the date of construction provides the most important clue; he worked out an ingenious method for pinpointing that date. He reasoned that one of the many problems facing the mysterious mastermind was how to ensure that his tunnellers, working inland from Smith's Cove, kept on a straight line so as to run smack into the Money Pit. That line is 14° south of the true east-west line. Surely, according to Furneaux, he would have given his men, who were presumably working in dim light deep underground, one of the clearly marked cardinal points of the compass (west). If so, the magnetic variation west of north at the time must have been 14°. The magnetic values for Nova Scotia go back to 1750 and can be estimated for much earlier periods. It is thought that Oak Island would have recorded that particular variation in about 1611. It seems pretty certain that it did so in 1780.

Who would have wanted to conceal something of great value on Oak Island in 1780? The answer lies in the world around Oak Island in that year. General Sir Henry Clinton, commander-in-chief of the British forces in America, had been installed in his headquarters at New York for two years. The year of his appointment, 1778, witnessed France's entry into the war on the side of the colonists, and the combined threat to New York from the French fleet and Washington's army was very real. Clinton's fall-back position, should he have had to evacuate New York, was Halifax, about 40 miles (64 kilometres) north of Oak Island. Is it not reasonable to suppose, asked Furneaux, that at some point during these perilous years Clinton may have seized on the idea of removing to a safe place some of the huge quantities of specie (money for the conduct of the war) in his keeping? If so, an island in Mahone Bay, which was en route should he have had to fall back on Halifax, would make sense. Moreover, a friend and colleague of Clinton's, John Montrésor, had surveyed Mahone Bay some years earlier. Perhaps Montrésor suggested the site.

So, according to this theory, some time around 1780 a contingent of British sappers,

led by an unknown engineer of rare genius, descended on Oak Island and performed their great work. The shattering implication of this for generations of treasure seekers is that the money, if it was actually deposited there (the hiding place could have formed part of a contingency plan that was not put into operation), must have been recovered by those who had hidden it, since there is no record of Clinton's having to explain away a few missing millions when he returned to England.

How could such a recovery have been effected, given the Money Pit's fool-proof system of flooding? For years searchers had tried in vain to locate flood gates, which they reckoned the designer must have installed to enable him to shut off the water when he returned. A blind alley, according to Furneaux – and so, in effect, was the Money Pit itself. Furneaux suggests that after the Money Pit and the tunnels had been dug (but not connected), one or more branch tunnels were run outwards and upwards from the Money Pit; at the end of those upward-reaching tunnels, probably not far beneath the surface of the ground, the treasure was concealed. Then the Money pit was filled in, the flood tunnels were connected to it, and the treasure was thereby completely safeguarded. Only he who knew its precise location could find it (and perhaps he could do so without bothering to excavate the Money Pit). All others would flounder in the watery swamp of the Money Pit forever.

It must be admitted that this solution to the puzzle has a weightiness about it that is alien to the old skull-and-crossbones tradition. But before assenting to it too quickly, it is appropriate to ask whether it accounts for all the evidence. How, for example, does it make sense of the metal objects encountered by the drilling operations of 1849 and 1897? And what about that piece of parchment with the tantalising inscription 'v.i.'?

Top: Sir Henry Clinton, commander-in-chief of the British forces in America from 1778 to 1782, who may have been responsible for the Money Pit. According to one theory, Clinton ordered his miners and engineers (above) to build the pit as a hiding place for some of the war funds in his keeping

Right: tourists listen to the story of the Money Pit, of the generations of hopeful prospectors who searched for what they believed to be a fortune at the bottom of the pit – and of the mystery that still surrounds it

THE MONEY PIT
TREASURE SEEKERS HAVE FOUND:
EVERY 10 FEET A PLATFORM OF LOGS
40 FEET A TIER OF CHARCOAL
50 FEET STONES WITH NUMBERS
60 FEET MANILLA GRASS
70 FEET RIND OF COCONUT
80 FEET TIER OF PUTTY
93 FEET THE WARNING STONE

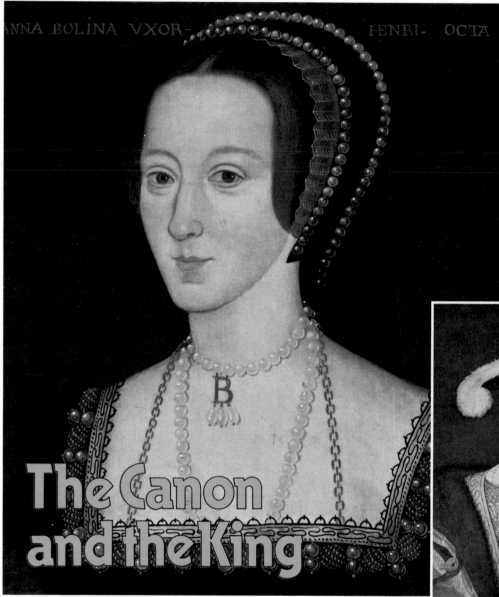

ANNA BOLINA VXOR— · · · HENRI · OCTA

The Canon and the King

Henry VIII died in 1547 at the end of a career darkened by many acts of greed and cruelty. LYNN PICKNETT recounts the story of a 20th-century churchman who believed he had brought Henry's spirit to repentance

IN 1917 A BRITISH MISSIONARY in China happened to read a biography of Anne Boleyn, second wife of Henry VIII, who was executed for adultery in 1536. The missionary was William Pakenham-Walsh, later a canon of Peterborough Cathedral. He was at first merely interested in Anne's life but gradually became immersed in the subject, which soon became a life-long passion. On his return to England, he determined to rescue the reputation of 'a Queen who has been much misunderstood'. But he soon found himself drawn into the afterlife agonies of Henry VIII himself, as communicated to well-known mediums and often in the presence of the clergyman.

The experiences of Pakenham-Walsh were related in *A Tudor story*, which was published in 1963, three years after his death at the age of 92. It is a bizarre yet poignant story. The author's sincerity, integrity and simplicity are strongly evident throughout. He himself had no psychic powers. He was a good-hearted, uncomplicated man who enjoyed cycling and brisk country walks. At seances, however, he broke almost every rule possible, divulging information in advance, and 'leading' the medium in obvious ways. Nevertheless, because of inner consistencies, certain circumstantial evidence and the clergyman's sense of purpose, the book is an intriguing and important contribution to psychical literature.

In August 1921 Pakenham-Walsh met a certain Mrs Clegg, a medium, at his sister's house. The first sitting set the pattern for many that followed over the next 12 years, involving several other mediums: a mixture of ingenuous 'leading' and reading between the lines by the Canon – and genuine but obscure 'evidence'. The spirit of a white-haired old man who appeared to Mrs Clegg was assumed by the Canon to be Anne Boleyn's father; a vague description of his daughter – 'with good hands, rather plump' – was, said the Canon, 'of course a perfect description of the Lady Anne' (despite the fact that Anne had six fingers on one hand).

Yet some of the information was confirmed later, after research. Queen Anne Boleyn did indeed have five brothers, whose names were correctly given by Mrs Clegg; and Anne had seriously quarrelled with her sister Mary, as the medium said. But Pakenham-Walsh then committed a major blunder by telling the medium who the spirit was – and had further meetings after that. One ended with Mrs Clegg saying that Anne foresaw how 'you will be offered a parish with the snowdrops and you will go to it with the daffodils.' Pakenham-Walsh was soon after appointed to the parish of Sulgrave in Northamptonshire, carpeted with snow-drops on his first visit and ablaze with daffodils when he took up residence. The gardener said he had 'never seen the like' in 40 years.

A need for forgiveness

If Anne Boleyn had restricted her 'visits' to Mrs Clegg the story might never have developed further. In December 1922, however, Pakenham-Walsh received a letter from Miss Eleanor Kelly, a Christian psychic. In her daily session of automatic writing, she said, she had received a message in which were mentioned both the Canon and Mr Frederick Bligh Bond, the eminent architect and 'psychic archaeologist'. She added: 'I

The chapel of St Peter ad Vincula (St Peter in chains), at the Tower of London, is Anne Boleyn's burial place. Her remains lie beneath the left-hand end of the altar. William Pakenham-Walsh prayed here that Anne, by whom he had become fascinated, 'might be to me a guardian angel'. He decided that he would write a play about her tragic life. It was not long afterwards that she first communicated with him – as he believed – at a seance

William Pakenham-Walsh was still a parson when he first received messages that he believed to come from Anne Boleyn. In due course he became a canon of Peterborough Cathedral – where, he noted, there was a shrine to Henry VIII's first wife, Katherine of Aragon. Did his devotion to the memory of Anne Boleyn cause him to misinterpret the evidence that came out of the sittings? Or did it mark him as the ideal recipient for the dead queen's urgent appeal for help?

have had some communication now and again with souls who have died in the same period as Henry VIII, and I am very much interested in the reference [in her script] to him and the Lady Anne and the need . . . for forgiveness on her part and reparation on his.'

She later received another message, this time from 'Alwyn, once a Thane of Sussex'. It spelled out the task at hand:

As all who touch the lives of others intimately must at least remove *all* that obstructs their unity, so must these two souls be cleared each alone, and each in unison, before they too take their places in the great structure of the Body of Christ. Anne has even still some shadows to let fall before her vision is clear; he, Henry, is but now beginning to be vaguely conscious of his need of cleansing.

To this end Mr Bond arranged for the Canon to meet one of the most famous mediums of the day, Mrs Hester Dowden, at her home in Chelsea, London. The seance took the form of automatic writing with the word Katherine repeated several times. The pencil then wrote: 'I want you to help someone who needs help from your world.' They obeyed instructions to move to a nearby house so that better 'contact' could be made. There, Mrs Dowden's pencil flew violently across her writing pad: 'I am here – HENRY REX.' They had, the Canon believed, made contact with the King through Katherine of Aragon, his first wife.

Using Mrs Dowden as amanuensis, Mr Bond and Miss Kelly talked to the monarch. Asked if he knew he was dead, Henry replied: 'Yes, I know. It has been but a nightmare. . . . I want to be told exactly what has happened and why I am still in a dark place. I feel as if I was back again in the earth.' He said that his daughter Elizabeth (whose mother was Anne Boleyn) meant nothing to him. When told she had become a great ruler, he answered acidly: 'I did not expect it from her mother's child.' Reminded that the divine right of kings would carry no weight on Judgement Day, Henry erupted: 'I shall not listen to *you*. You are a fool. I would have had you executed in my time.' And the information that England's current king was George V caused a further outburst: 'I care not. You are a varlet; some knave from a tavern who is making sport of me because I lie at your mercy.' Veering from self-reproach to self-pity to outbursts of rage, he finally agreed to pray for forgiveness, but added: 'I will not pray here. A king prays alone.'

Henry, it appeared, was in the grip of great inner conflict caused by his actions as king. It seemed that he would need to forgive and be forgiven by other souls from his lifetime, such as Cardinal Thomas Wolsey and Henry's third Queen, Jane Seymour. Historians generally believe that she was his favourite wife, yet the King's spirit ranted that he detested her. This hatred seemed to be the main obstacle to his own spiritual

progress. The Canon felt particularly pleased, therefore, when he and the mediums effected a reconciliation between the spirits of Henry and Jane.

Of Henry's six wives it was his first, Katherine of Aragon, who claimed him as husband and who wrote, through Miss Kelly: 'Love is guiding him along the upward, rugged path.' It is clear, however, that Henry's desire to be helped began in earnest when Pakenham-Walsh told him that if he repented his sins he would be reunited with his sons – Henry, who died after six weeks (but who, it was claimed, had since grown up in the afterlife), and Edward, who had reigned from 1547 to 1553.

The Canon's greatest day was 24 June 1933 when, in the company of two mediums, Mrs Heber-Percy and Mrs Theo Monson, he was told that he was in the presence not

Katherine of Aragon, the first wife of Henry VIII, had many children by him, but only one, the future Mary I, survived. Henry's anxiety to divorce Katherine in order to marry Anne Boleyn and secure the succession led to England's break with Rome and the establishment of the Anglican Church. Katherine refused to recognise the annulment enacted by Thomas Cranmer, the new Archbishop of Canterbury – and was allegedly still obdurate 400 years after her death

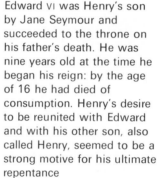

Edward VI was Henry's son by Jane Seymour and succeeded to the throne on his father's death. He was nine years old at the time he began his reign: by the age of 16 he had died of consumption. Henry's desire to be reunited with Edward and with his other son, also called Henry, seemed to be a strong motive for his ultimate repentance

only of Henry and his Queens, Wolsey, Sir Thomas More, Elizabeth I and others, but also the spirits of his own daughter Helen and his son Willy. Henry wished it to be made public that he repented of his misdeeds. Anne Boleyn said that 'the manuscript [of *A Tudor story*] is one of the ladders from here to you and from you to us, by which many may climb to true knowledge.' The Canon pronounced a blessing on the gathering, seen and unseen, and then the visitors were gone.

A prayer answered

If one believes that the soul can survive death and that even the most evil man can be helped to progress in the afterlife, then the child-like honest Canon would seem eminently suitable to 'rescue' the arrogant Henry.

Critics, however, would find it all too easy to tear the story apart. Although none of the mediums knew Pakenham-Walsh before they met, they would almost certainly have heard of his obsession with the Tudors. A sensitive could, even if unconsciously, have picked up telepathic impressions of his desire to be Anne Boleyn's champion and of his exalted image of Anne. It is natural, too, that Pakenham-Walsh should have wanted to help Henry, a tortured soul in search of redemption. It is significant that Henry's first wife, Katherine, sought earthly help for him. In the Canon's eyes, she was probably Henry's only legal wife. Although a number of 'tests' set by Anne were seized upon by Pakenham-Walsh as evidence of her survival, it could also be said that they proved only that he was ignorant of the modern theory of general (super) ESP.

Anne Boleyn had said on the scaffold in 1536: 'I pray God to save the King.' Could, perhaps, a gentle ex-missionary have been chosen to answer her prayer 400 years later?

Prisoner without a face

For over 200 years the European imagination has been haunted by the legend of a prisoner condemned by Louis XIV to spend his life masked and in solitude. SIMON INNES reveals the true history of the man behind the mask

AT THREE O'CLOCK IN THE AFTERNOON of Thursday 18 September 1698, a new governor of the Bastille prison, Monsieur de Saint-Mars, arrived in Paris. In his litter he brought with him a man known only as the 'ancient prisoner', whose face was hidden by a black velvet mask fastened at the neck by iron clasps. He had been in the custody of Saint-Mars for no less than 29 years.

When the prisoner died five years later, he was buried in the night, under a false name.

Above: the myth of the man in the iron mask – doomed perpetually to wear a heavy helmet and manacles. In reality he was not kept in fetters, and his mask was of velvet, with iron clasps

Below: Pinerolo, the citadel where the man in the mask was first imprisoned

For 34 years no one around him had mentioned his true name, he had been kept from the sight of anyone who might recognise him, and he had been strictly prevented from speaking to his gaolers.

Not one of these afflictions was remarkable in itself. Many prisoners of Louis XIV were kept incommunicado – some were even required to wear masks. All were buried anonymously. Ministers who had been dismissed from their posts in the government, royal envoys who had for some reason failed to bring negotiations to a successful conclusion, courtiers who had killed a man in a duel – anyone could find himself in a royal prison and, unless he was returned to favour, die there.

But there were strange rumours about this particular prisoner. Eight years after his death Madame Palatine, sister-in-law of Louis XIV, wrote to the Electress Sophia of Hanover, mother of the future George I of England:

> He was an English lord who had been mixed up in the Duke of Berwick's affair against King William. He was treated thus so that the king might never know what became of him.

This could not be true. William of Orange did not accede to the English throne until 1689, when the prisoner had been in Saint-Mars's custody for some 20 years. This rumour had clearly been encouraged by Louis to obscure the true identity of the man in the mask.

The philosopher and writer Voltaire thought that he had come nearer the truth. He was twice imprisoned in the Bastille, in 1717 and 1726, and could have spoken to prisoners and gaolers who knew the 'ancient prisoner'. In 1738 he wrote to the Abbé Dubois: 'I am fairly well informed on the adventure of the man in the iron mask.'

This is the first mention of an *iron* mask; the legend took root firmly. In 1771 Voltaire alleged that the mysterious prisoner was a half-brother of Louis XIV, imprisoned because he threatened Louis's Crown.

From that time, the myth grew apace – especially after the publication of Alexandre

have the man named Eustache Dauger sent to Pignerol. It is of the utmost importance to His service that he should be most securely guarded and that he should in no way give information about himself nor send letters to anyone at all. I am informing you of this in advance so that you can have a cell prepared in which you will place him securely, taking care that the windows of the place in which he is put do not give on to any place that can be approached by anyone, and that there are double doors to be shut, for your guards not to hear anything. You must yourself take to him, once a day, the day's necessities, and you must never listen, under any pretext whatever, to what he may want to reveal to you, always threatening to kill him if he ever opens his mouth to speak of anything but his day-to-day needs.

This letter was dated 19 July 1669. On the same day Louvois wrote to de Vauroy, military governor of the town of Dunkirk, which was temporarily an English possession. The letter called de Vauroy away from

Above: the fortress of the Bastille, in Paris, as it was in the 18th century. The prisoner in the mask died here in 1703. The governor of the Bastille, Saint-Mars (inset), had been the custodian of the man in the mask for some 34 years. Whenever Saint-Mars was appointed to a new post, he would take his prisoner along with him

Left: Louis XIV, portrayed as the commander of the French army, trampling down the enemies of France. Among these, presumably, was counted the unfortunate prisoner in the mask – but his offence is still not known with certainty

Dumas's world-famous novel on which many romances and films were to be based. Only after the fall of the French monarchy in 1789 and the gradual disclosure of the state archives did it become possible to trace the history of the 'ancient prisoner'.

In 1664 Saint-Mars, a former under-officer of the Musketeers, was appointed governor of the prison in the fortress at Pinerolo (or Pignerol), in Piedmont, north-western Italy. Pinerolo was then in the kingdom of Savoy, but the French occupied the fortress under the terms of the Treaty of Cherasco of 1631.

Some five years after his appointment, Saint-Mars received a letter from the French Minister of War, the Marquis de Louvois:

The King has commanded that I am to

Left: Voltaire – dramatist, poet, philosopher and wit – was one of the first writers to elaborate on the story of the prisoner in the mask. His fanciful account, full of inconsistencies and errors, proposed the idea that the prisoner was an illegitimate half-brother of Louis XIV, the result of infidelity by Louis XIII's queen

the duties that normally occupied him:

I am informed that officers of the Spanish troops are pursuing deserters on the King's territory. . . . His Majesty desires that you are to attack these officers who come into conflict with our troops when they are seizing their deserters.

And to the civil governor of Dunkirk he wrote: 'As M. de Vauroy has business which requires him to absent himself, I beg you very kindly to give him leave.'

But a very different mission was intended for de Vauroy. It seems likely that at this date news had been received that Dauger was about to arrive in Dunkirk on a ship from England, and that arrangements were being made well in advance for his arrest and imprisonment.

This is indicated by the date of the letter of authorisation instructing de Vauroy to

Above: de Louvois, Louis XIV's ruthless Minister of War, who issued a stream of harsh orders concerning the 'ancient prisoner'

Left: the popular notion of the man in the iron mask has found its way into novels, plays, films and music. This affecting scene embellished the cover of a 19th-century song sheet

Below: Nicolas Fouquet was a fellow-prisoner of the man in the mask. This portrait shows him while still a powerful statesman

Below right: d'Artagnan, who escorted Nicolas Fouquet to Pinerolo, was linked forever with the masked prisoner by Dumas in one of his romances of the three musketeers

through with my sword. On my life, I shall not fail to observe, very punctiliously, your commands.

There is no doubt whatsoever, then, that a man of considerable importance named Eustache Dauger was arrested in the vicinity of Dunkirk some time between 19 and 28 July 1669, and by 21 August was safely incarcerated in the dungeon of the fortress of Pinerolo.

The most important of the prisoners who were already in captivity at Pinerolo was Nicolas Fouquet, the disgraced Minister of Finance. He had been an extremely powerful statesman during the troubled years between the death of Louis XIII in 1643 and the assumption of active government by Louis XIV at the age of 21, in 1660. He was a member of a secret society – the Company of the Holy Sacrament, known usually as *la Compagnie* – which exercised incalculable influence during this time. He was very close to Cardinal Mazarin, who shaped the destiny of France at the beginning of the new reign.

Committed for life

Fouquet became Minister of Finance in 1653 and had hoped to become prime minister, but his former friend Jean-Baptiste Colbert rapidly destroyed his reputation with the King by drawing attention to all sorts of irregularities in the accounts. On 20 December 1664, Fouquet was committed for life into the custody of Saint-Mars. Four weeks later, guarded by 100 musketeers under the command of d'Artagnan – destined to be the hero of a succession of Dumas novels – he arrived at Pinerolo. The King had written to Saint-Mars:

With respect to the form and manner according to which the said Captain de Saint-Mars will have to guard the said Fouquet, His Majesty does not prescribe any, relying entirely on his prudent and wise conduct and on what he saw practised by M. d'Artagnan during all the time he guarded him both at the Bois de Vincennes and at the Bastille; His Majesty only recommends

convey Eustache Dauger to Pinerolo. It was issued on 28 July, only nine days after de Vauroy was supposedly assigned to deal with intruding Spanish troops. A smokescreen had been laid down over Dauger's arrest – even before it had occurred.

The arrival of the prisoner at Pinerolo was confirmed by a letter from Saint-Mars to Louvois, dated 21 August:

M. de Vauroy has handed over to me the man named Eustache d'Auger. As soon as I had put him in a very secure place, while waiting for the cell I am having prepared for him to be completed, I told him in the presence of M. de Vauroy that if he should speak to me or anyone else of anything other than his day-to-day needs, I would run him

very expressly to Captain de Saint-Mars not to allow the said Fouquet to communicate with anyone by word or by writing or to be visited by anyone or to leave his apartment for any cause or under any pretext whatever, not even to take a walk.

Fouquet was to be allowed a confessor, but he was to be chosen by Saint-Mars and his visits were restricted to four per year.

When Dauger was admitted to the prison nearly five years later, Louvois wrote:

You can give a prayer book to your new prisoner, and if he asks you for any other give it him also. You can let him hear on Sundays and Feast Days the mass that is said for M. Fouquet, without, however, being at the same place, and you will see that he is so well guarded during that time that he cannot escape or speak to anyone; you can even let him have confession three or four times a year, if he so wishes, and no more unless he should contract some mortal illness.

It is easy to deduce from this that, as a prisoner, Dauger was equal in importance to Fouquet. The insistence on his total isolation

Right: the masked prisoner tries to send a message to the outside world. According to Voltaire, he scratched a message on a silver plate with a knife, and flung the plate from a window. But it was found by an illiterate fisherman, who obligingly returned it to the prison governor

Below: the mysterious prisoner dines with his custodian on the journey to his last prison, the Bastille. Only the governor's pistol, lying within easy reach, reveals that this is no ordinary social occasion

suggests that he was a direct threat to the security of the realm, or that he knew something so dangerous that he had to be kept from all contact with others.

If Saint-Mars had any difficulty in maintaining sufficient secrecy concerning his prisoner, his problems must have increased in November 1671, when he took charge of another important prisoner. This was the Comte de Lauzun, formerly Captain of the King's Bodyguard. Louvois ordered that Lauzun was to be imprisoned with a single valet and was never to be allowed to leave the prison or communicate with anybody. On 9 December 1671, Saint-Mars wrote:

I will lodge him in the two vaulted chambers that are over those of M. Fouquet: these are the ones with the barred windows that you yourself examined. . . . The place is so constructed that I can have holes made, through which I can spy into the apartment. I shall also know all that he does and says through the valet whom I will furnish as you have ordered. I have found one with much trouble, for the clever ones do not wish to pass their lives in prison. . . .

In 1675 Fouquet's valet, La Rivière, became seriously ill with dropsy and was not always able to serve his master. In reply to a request from Saint-Mars, Louvois wrote:

His Majesty approves that you give, as valet to M. Fouquet, the prisoner whom M. de Vauroy brought to you; but whatever may happen, you must refrain from placing him with M. de Lauzun, or with anyone else. . . .

The implication of this is that Fouquet

would already be in possession of whatever secrets Dauger knew. It also suggests that Dauger was of nowhere near the same social standing as Fouquet – unless he was being deliberately humiliated.

Louvois wrote directly to Fouquet on several subsequent occasions, stressing that Dauger must not be allowed to converse with La Rivière, his other valet. However, when Fouquet died in 1680 this prohibition must have been forgotten, for the two valets were locked up together.

Lauzun, the other important prisoner, was aware of Dauger's existence: he had contrived to make a hole through a fireplace into Fouquet's cell. But after his release from Pinerolo in 1682 he seems never to have spoken or written of Eustache Dauger, with whom he had been incarcerated for 10 years.

In 1681 Saint-Mars received a promotion: he was appointed to the governorship of

the fortress of Exiles, a prison some 30 miles (50 kilometres) distant from Pinerolo. Two particularly important prisoners accompanied Saint-Mars, their safe custody being of the utmost importance to the King – and from the correspondence of the time it is clear that they were Dauger and La Rivière.

The two prisoners were placed under even greater security than at Pinerolo: their rooms were watched over by sentries day and night, and for confessor they were allowed only a very old priest who lived some distance away.

In January 1687 Saint-Mars wrote to Louvois to inform him that the prisoner who had been sick – La Rivière – had died. In his reply Louvois informed Saint-Mars of his appointment to the prison on the island of Ste Marguerite in the Bay of Cannes and instructed him to convey the 'ancient prisoner' there in secrecy.

It was while Dauger was in the prison at Ste Marguerite, if we are to believe Voltaire, that he scratched a message with a knife on a silver plate and flung it from a window. It was picked up by a fisherman – who took it to Saint-Mars. The prison governor asked him if he had read what was on the plate. When the fisherman replied that he could not read, Saint-Mars remarked that it was lucky for him that he could not, and dismissed him.

On 1 March 1698 Saint-Mars was again promoted, this time to the governorship of the Bastille. He was to come with his ancient prisoner, 'taking all precautions to prevent his being seen or recognised by anyone'.

It was on the journey from Ste Marguerite to Paris that the mask made its first recorded appearance: from that time on the prisoner wore it continually until he died.

Above: the prison on the island of Sainte Marguerite, where the man in the mask spent 11 years. The window of his cell is the third from the right. It was from here that he threw the plate bearing a message

Right: the legend of the iron mask has been heavily embroidered in fiction. In this scene from a London theatre production of 1899, the cell has become rather crowded: the prisoner has the company of a gaoler, a beautiful girl, a noble visitor – and a corpse

Many identities have been proposed for the prisoner in the mask. Many reasons for his long imprisonment have been suggested. Historical evidence disposes of most of them, but the most perplexing mysteries remain

Left: Louis XIII is often linked with the masked prisoner. Was the prisoner the bastard son of the King, and therefore a grave threat to the legitimate son, Louis XIV?

Below: Anne of Austria who, after 14 childless years, bore a son to Louis XIII. One theory suggests that Louis was not the father of the child, who was to become Louis XIV. Years later, one of the illegitimate King's half-brothers had to be kept quiet – and became the prisoner in the mask

Poisoner, priest or pretender?

THE 'ANCIENT PRISONER' who died in the Bastille in 1703 was undoubtedly called Eustache Dauger. This was established in 1890 by Jules Lair, who traced the prisoner's career back to his arrest in 1669. Lair's work put paid to what had until then been the most plausible of the theories concerning the man in the iron mask.

This theory hinged on the false name under which the prisoner's burial was recorded: de Marchiel, or Marchioly. It was known that one Ercole Mattioli, secretary to the Duke of Mantua, had been imprisoned in Pinerolo in 1679 and there was no other record that could be interpreted as referring to his death. It seemed logical, then, to identify Mattioli with the man in the mask –

Above: the masked prisoner, dressed in the finest clothes, and heavily guarded even in his cell. This picture is as fanciful as the story it illustrates – *The man in the iron mask*, by Alexandre Dumas, which did so much to shape the legend

even though there was no secret about Mattioli's imprisonment. However, now that it is known that the prisoner was Dauger, who was imprisoned in 1669, and since we can now follow his movements up to his death, it is clear that he was not Mattioli.

Another suspect had been James de la Roche, who represented himself to the Jesuits in Rome as an illegitimate son of Charles II. He was supposedly sent on a secret mission to London in the spring of 1669, under the name of the Abbé Pregnani. However, he died in the summer of that year – just when the man in the mask was beginning his long imprisonment.

There was indeed a real Abbé Pregnani, and he was himself in London at this time:

Eustache Dauger was one Martin, valet of Paul Roux de Marsilly, a man who was involved in a Protestant intrigue and executed in Paris in June 1669. The Foreign Minister had written to the French ambassador in London, asking him to persuade Martin to return to France for the trial of his master. However, there is also in existence a letter from Louvois, the Minister of War, dated 13 July 1669, stating that the valet's evidence is no longer needed, and that he is therefore not required to return.

It was in 1930 that a historian, Maurice Duvivier, searching the Bibliothèque Nationale in Paris, uncovered a real Eustache Dauger. He had been born in 1637, the third son of François Auger de Cavoye and Marie de Lort de Sérignan. The father, captain of the guard to Cardinal Richelieu, came from a minor landowning family in Picardy; his wife was from the Languedoc and had been a young widow when he married her.

There were 11 children altogether – six boys and five girls. Four of the sons had been killed in the service of the King by the time of Dauger's arrest in 1669, but Eustache's younger brother Louis lived until 1715, becoming Marquis de Cavoye and Grand Maréchal des Logis de la Maison du Roi (superintendent of the king's household).

Eustache was a year older than Louis XIV, and as children the two knew one another well in the inner circles of the court. His other playmates included Philip Mancini, the nephew of Cardinal Mazarin, who was a friend of the family, and the future Duc de Lauzun, who was later to be incarcerated with him in the prison at Pinerolo.

By the year 1654, when he was still only 17, Eustache had become the eldest surviving son, with the death in battle of both his elder brothers. But as soon as he reached his majority, Eustache seems to have become involved in a succession of unsavoury episodes, including a black mass and the killing

an astrologer and intriguer, he had been sent there to spy on Charles II. He arrived in February and met the King a few days later, but he failed to impress him. As Charles wrote to his sister:

> I came from Newmarket the day before yesterday. . . . L'Abbé Pregnani was there most of the time and I believe will give you some account of it, but not that he lost his money upon confidence that the stars could tell which horse would win, for he had the bad luck to foretell three times wrong and Monmouth had such faith in him that he lost his money.

The Abbé was recalled to France on 17 July, but any possibility that he was the man arrested in Dunkirk a few days later is disposed of by the fact that he died in Rome in 1678 or 1679.

In his book *The valet's tragedy* the English folklorist Andrew Lang suggested that

Above: Louis XIII and his foremost subject, Cardinal Richelieu, kneel at the feet of Christ. Among the Cardinal's services to his king were strenuous efforts to ensure that France was provided with an heir to the throne. The masked prisoner may have met his fate because he knew a state secret – the identity of Louis XIV's true father

Right: the young Louis XIV. One of his playmates was Eustache Dauger, son of Richelieu's captain of the guard. Louis became absolute monarch: Dauger may have been his victim, the prisoner in the mask

of a court page. In 1664 his mother disinherited him, and in 1665 he was forced to sell his commission.

We now have an outline portrait of the man in the mask: a young man of good family, a childhood friend of the King, who has grown increasingly dissolute and spendthrift and by the age of 30 has fallen on hard times. But this does not explain the long punishment that he was subsequently to endure. When his younger brother Louis, later to become a distinguished member of the court, was sent to the Bastille for killing a man in a duel, he served only four years. What could Eustache have done that could merit not only 34 years in prison, but also exceedingly stringent measures to conceal his identity?

There is reason to suspect that he was engaged in espionage. He was probably returning from England when he was arrested in Dunkirk. Charles II was engaged in secret and tortuous negotiations with Louis XIV, hoping to obtain French money to support the re-establishment of a Catholic monarchy in England. Clandestine agents regularly went back and forth between the two courts.

In December 1667 Charles had written to his sister Minette, the sister-in-law of Louis:

> You know how much secrecy is necessary for the carrying out of the business and I assure you that nobody does or shall know anything of it but myself and *that one person more*, till it be fit to be public.

A year later, in January 1669, he wrote:

Above: the English king, Charles II, engaged in intrigues with Louis XIV in an attempt to get French money. Eustache Dauger may have been used as an agent in the negotiations between the two monarchs

> I had written thus far when I received yours by the Italian whose name and capacity you do not know, and he delivered your letter to me in a passage where it was so dark as I should not know his face again if I saw him.

Could this 'Italian' have been Dauger? It is strange, but not impossible, that Charles should have thought him to be an Italian. A mission of such delicacy could have suited Eustache Dauger well. Known to everyone at court as a personable, swashbuckling ex-officer, his movements between the French and English courts would not arouse suspicion. Being desperately in need of funds, he was just the sort of man likely to be recruited as an agent.

Doctor of death

However, at about this time there was a certain 'surgeon d'Auger' who has been identified – by Maurice Duvivier, who carried out so much of the investigation into Eustache's life – with the man in the mask. This d'Auger was involved with a gang of poisoners around 1670. If the man in the mask had once been a poisoner, an obscure postscript in a letter written by Louvois gains in interest. Louvois had written to Saint-Mars, governor of the prison at Pinerolo, shortly after the sudden death of Fouquet. Aged 65, Fouquet had been expecting a pardon from the King. Louvois wrote:

> Send me word how it happened that the man named Eustache has been able to

Recipe for evil

Maurice Duvivier, who identified the masked prisoner as Eustache Dauger, believed that he was the same man as a surgeon called d'Auger, who was named in a great poisoning scandal involving the nobility. The most eminent person to be implicated was Madame de Montespan, who, while a lady-in-waiting, had engaged in black masses in order to become Louis XIV's mistress – and had obtained her wish. She plunged deeper into blasphemous practices designed to retain the King's favour. When at last he tired of her in 1679 she tried to kill him by black magic. Her activities were exposed by Nicolas de la Reynie, chief of the Paris police, who had been investigating the widespread use of love charms and poisons by the nobility. Madame de Montespan was allowed to live: 36 other people were executed. One of these was Catherine Monvoisin (right), who became the most notorious magician arrested by La Reynie. D'Auger's name was cited in the trials of 1679 and 1680 – but he had disappeared 10 years before.

do what you sent me word of, and where he got the drugs necessary for the purpose. . . .

What had Dauger been doing with these drugs? Had he been trying to heal Fouquet? Or helping him on his way out of this life? As we shall see, there may have been a connection between Dauger and Fouquet that antedated their shared imprisonment in Pinerolo, and may have led to enmity between them.

Whatever the truth about the death of Fouquet, the question remains: why should a failed secret agent, or a convicted poisoner, have been treated with such severity and regarded as so important that no unauthorised person should be able to speak with him or catch a sight of his face? Could there be substance in the original rumour, retailed by Voltaire, that the prisoner was a half-brother of Louis XIV?

Most commentators have considered the possibility that Eustache Dauger was the

Below: the true end of the 'ancient prisoner': the certificate of his burial, under the name Marchioly, at the Bastille in 1703

Bottom: 'the skeleton in the iron mask' – supposedly found at the fall of the Bastille in 1789. This is yet another wholly fanciful detail in the legend

Richelieu prevailed on the captain of his personal guard to perform the act of which Louis XIII proved incapable.

The secret may have been known to Eustache and his brother Louis – and it was one that could topple the throne of France. Is the solution of the mystery of Eustache's incarceration simply that, penniless and increasingly dissolute, he had begun to talk? Had he tried to add substance to his insinuations by drawing attention to his family resemblance to the King? It is possible. Louis XIV, although determined to be an absolute monarch, may have drawn the line at ordering the execution of his half-brother.

But there is an additional fascinating possibility. It is suspected that Nicolas Fouquet, together with the priest who was later to be canonised as St Vincent de Paul and other members of *la Compagnie*, was conspiring to restore the Merovingian line, the dynasty that had been deposed from the French throne by the Carolingians in the seventh century. If Louis XIV's illegitimacy could be proved, and Eustache Dauger was prepared to bear witness, a Merovingian pretender stood a good chance of succeeding to the throne. Is this why Dauger, half-brother of the King, was shut away from converse with others, his face sometimes hidden in a mask, until, after 34 years, he died – and became a legend?

illegitimate son of Louis XIII. But the suggestion does not seem consistent with Madame de Cavoye's renowned fidelity. There is another intriguing possibility, however: that Louis XIV was himself the illegitimate son – of Dauger's father, François.

The birth of Louis XIV was 'unexpected, almost miraculous' (in the words of the *Cambridge modern history*). In 1637 Louis XIII and his queen, Anne of Austria, had been married for 22 years, but had lived apart for 14. They had no children and it was rumoured that the King was impotent.

Nevertheless, it was essential that an heir to the throne of France should be born, and Cardinal Richelieu, who was effectively the real ruler of France, began to arrange a reconciliation between the King and Queen. They met at one of Richelieu's houses in the country, and soon afterwards it was announced that the Queen was pregnant. The King's younger brother, the Duke of Orleans, who had hoped to succeed to the throne, was so sceptical of the news that he remarked that Richelieu must be the father.

The child that was born was a fine physical specimen, quite unlike Louis XIII. But we know that it was often remarked, a half-century later, how alike Louis XIV was to the Marquis de Cavoye, Eustache's younger brother Louis. It seems quite probable that

Under the greenwood tree

The greenwood has always been a place where strange things happen – a doorway from the real world into the beyond. And weird things still happen in woods – as in Clapham Wood on England's South Downs. HAMISH HOWARD and TOYNE NEWTON report

A hollow oak stands sentry to the village of Clapham – and to the forbidding Clapham Wood (inset), for hundreds of years the scene of weird incidents

CLAPHAM WOOD is a small densely-treed area nestling in the shelter of the South Downs in West Sussex, England. Travelling southwards, a sharp left turn off the busy road known as Long Furlong at Findon leads into this area of mystery and intrigue, of strange disappearances and UFO sightings. There is even an ancient hollow oak, which signposts the way to the village, adding to the general air of mystery. That there is 'something weird' in the woods has always been rumoured. But what that something is, no one seems to know.

On a hill above the village, as if protecting its parishioners from the dark woods beyond, stands the 13th-century Church of the Blessed Virgin Mary. The strange atmosphere of the woods themselves is felt immediately. Stunted trees twist and writhe as if in pain; there is a larger crater, believed to

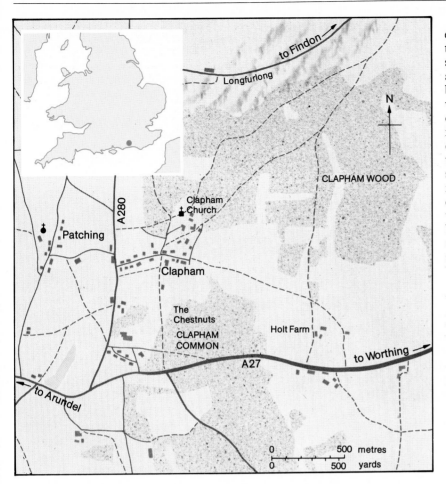

Above: the location of Clapham Wood

One such sighting concerns a telephone engineer who was driving home alone along the Findon Road after night duty when he saw a large saucer-shaped object in the sky above the woods. It hovered for some time before making a circle of the area, then veered off. That was in October 1972, when other sightings were independently reported in that area. One report came from a couple out walking near Long Furlong who thought they saw Jupiter or Venus low in the western sky – until it started to move very quickly due north, keeping in line with a ridge of the downs, as it came towards them. Suddenly, when the object was over Clapham Wood, a beam of light descended vertically from it, and then rapidly withdrew, and the object shot away north-eastwards at great speed. The beam was visible for about 10 seconds.

In fact the brief time the Clapham Wood UFOs are visible makes their verification almost impossible, as one inhabitant of the village found in 1968. It was 2 a.m. and, being unable to sleep, he was making himself a hot drink; glancing out of the kitchen window, he saw a saucer-shaped object hovering directly over the nearby woods. He promptly made an emergency call to the police; although the call was answered speedily, by the time the police arrived the UFO had disappeared.

By far the most significant sightings in this area are those reported by Paul Glover of the British Phenomenon Research Group, who was walking with a friend along the downs towards Clapham Wood one clear starlit night in the summer of 1967. At about 10 p.m. both suddenly became aware of a 'huge black mass' low in the sky blotting out the stars as it moved very quickly towards them.

The object was boomerang-shaped and made no sound. As it passed overhead the displacement of air was so great they ducked into the bushes for safety.

have been caused by a wartime bomb – although some maintain it was a meteorite and yet others say it is merely an ancient lime pit – where nothing grows; and there are mysterious little clearings containing ruins of old cottages.

Perhaps it was from one of these, a couple of centuries ago, that an old woman saw what would today be recognised as a UFO. She told villagers that one dark night she had seen a 'bright round shape like the full Moon' float down into the woods and disappear in the bushes.

The outcome of this event seems to have been that 'the woods were filled with fumes that stinketh of burning matter' and that many local folk thereafter were 'affeared to go there'. As for the old woman of the woods, she appears to have been immediately 'smitten of the palsy', and was given a wide berth by the locals; this may have been because of her sighting, but it seems more reasonable to suppose she was the victim of one of the witch hunts so prevalent in England at that time.

Since those far off days there have been many more UFO sightings – and some say landings – in the small area of Clapham Wood, and although several witnesses have given reports to the police there must be many people who are too afraid of ridicule to do so. The fact that these sightings often occur at night when few witnesses are about makes them very difficult to prove.

Below: Mr R. D. Bennett, warden of Clapham church, whose rector disappeared in Clapham Wood in 1979. Mr Bennett comments that the villagers think the wood is 'extremely weird'

They vehemently denied it could have been a cloud, for it retained its shape, was on a definite course, and there was no wind to drive it – certainly not at the tremendous speed at which it was travelling. Somewhat shaken they continued their walk, and minutes later saw two bright objects high in the sky, which they watched for several minutes. One of the UFOs released a smaller object that travelled across to the second object, seemed to enter it, and then re-emerged and veered off, disappearing from sight.

There was no denying that that night there was increased UFO activity in the area for some reason, but it was when Paul Glover and his companion were approaching Clapham Wood about an hour later that the most spectacular sighting occurred. Two yellow lights descended in the region of the woods, followed just a few seconds later by two more, and then a final pair, making a total of three groups of two. Then at the point where they seemed to have dipped down into the woods, two white beams of light shot out horizontally – quite unimpeded by the contours of the downlands – followed by the next two beams and then the final two, all travelling very fast, before disappearing into the night sky. No craft of any kind could be seen behind the lights.

Messages from a ouija board

During that same year, in the village of Rustington a few miles westwards along the coast, two schoolboys, Toyne Newton and John Arnold, who had never even heard of Clapham Wood, had a strange story spelled out to them on a ouija board: that Clapham Wood was a base for spacecraft, and that one

Paul Glover saw UFOs in Clapham Wood – a huge black boomerang (above) followed by small lights moving at speed (below)

had landed recently to fetch supplies of sulphur and other chemicals.

No one believed the boys, of course, but nearly 10 years later an investigation was carried out when soil samples were taken from the woods. From the report given in BBC-TV's *Nationwide* programme at the time it seems there was more than a grain of truth at least in the boys' sulphur story.

The investigation had actually been triggered off by reports of dogs disappearing in the woods in 1975. According to a local newspaper, the *Worthing Herald*, Wallace, a three-year-old chow belonging to Mr and Mrs Peter Love of Clapham, disappeared, as did a two-year-old collie belonging to Mr John Cornford. Apparently the collie, although normally obedient, suddenly rushed off into a small copse between two trees in an area known locally as the Chestnuts, and was never seen again – although its mystified owner searched the place thoroughly.

Mrs H. T. Wells, who lives at nearby Durrington, said that when her collie gets near the woods it 'becomes desperate', and a golden retriever belonging to Mr E. F. Rawlins of Worthing ran into the woods one day and returned 'very distressed'. Shortly afterwards it became paralysed and the vet had to destroy it.

Another dog owner, who wishes to remain anonymous, reported that when she took her dog to this area it ran round in circles foaming at the mouth, with its eyes bulging

out of its head as if in great pain, and only with difficulty did she manage to entice it back into her car and drive home, where the dog eventually calmed down.

This part of the woods is easily accessible to the public, being on the A27 dual carriageway, and it is regularly used for exercising dogs. It is also used by horse riders. One young horseman (who wishes to remain anonymous) tethered his mount firmly to a tree stump while he relieved himself in the woods, and was amazed to find the animal had disappeared during his brief absence. Although he searched the area extensively and made exhaustive enquiries, the horse was never found.

Animals are not alone in being affected by the peculiar atmosphere in this particular part of the woods, for several people have described how they have felt 'pushed over by invisible forces', while others have felt faint for no apparent reason.

Two men walking together in the woods told how they were both suddenly afflicted at the same time – one doubling over in agony and staggering, the other clutching at his head and saying that he felt as if his eardrums 'were being pulled from the inside outwards'. These painful effects disappeared simultaneously when the two men had gone about 50 yards (45 metres) further.

It seems beyond doubt that this small area encapsulates a source of electrical charge, or ray, or unknown force, which, when released into the atmosphere in small bursts, seems to affect anyone in the vicinity at the time with some kind of abnormal pressure or even mild apoplexy. But what the force is, no one seems to know.

Its strange and disturbing effects seem to be metamorphic, for – according to the local press – the body of a man who went missing in the woods was found only two weeks later in such an advanced state of decomposition

Above: Clapham Wood's mysterious crater. Nothing will grow there; no one knows its cause

Over: the strange black shape seen in Clapham Wood by Dave Stringer in 1977. He later found a footprint at the site (above right) – similar to one he had seen at the meeting place of a black coven in Brighton

Below: Mr John Cornford, a local farmer, whose two-year-old collie dog went missing in Clapham Wood and was never seen again

that only when the body was positively identified could the short time lapse be pinpointed. Forensic evidence showed that the normally accepted rate of a decomposing corpse had, in this particular case, been greatly accelerated due to some unknown factor.

Mystifying reports such as these have a double effect in that, while keeping apprehensive people away, those given to seeking the truth of such situations are particularly drawn to the area. Among these is Dave Stringer of the Southern Paranormal Investigation Group, who, while not disbelieving the reports of so many independent witnesses, nevertheless visited the woods in August of 1977 'with an open mind' – and his Geiger counter.

He was aware of a strange silence, but the woods were beautiful and the air still as he came to the part called the Chestnuts. Everything appeared normal, but as he walked through the heavy undergrowth he had to raise the Geiger counter above his head. It was then that it began to register at an alarming rate before returning to normal.

Wonderingly, Stringer looked back at the area through which he had just passed, and saw a dark shape about 12 feet (3.5 metres) in height; while not being distinctive in outline, it was very definitely not smoke, or a smoke-enshrouded bush, but he could describe it only as a 'black mass'. Seconds later a large white disc shot out from behind nearby trees at an angle of about 45° and disappeared into the sky, and simultaneously the dark form disappeared also.

Stringer retraced his steps, not using the Geiger counter this time but looking down at the ground, which was part grass and part muddy footpath, for some evidence of a solid shape to back up what he thought he had witnessed. At the spot where the form had appeared he came upon a faint imprint of a four-toed foot, twice the width of a man's foot but very narrow at the heel.

Only on one other occasion had he seen such a mysterious footprint, and that had been at Devil's Dyke near Brighton, where there was known to be a black magic coven. Could there be a connection?

Devil's footprint?

Part of a black coven's ritual involves the burning of sulphur, which could account for the acrid smell and fumes reported in the woods, and one particular branch of their rumoured experimentation concerns the dematerialisation of small creatures. This, it is claimed, releases the creatures' 'life spark', which escapes without form or shape.

Stringer made a quick sketch of the single footprint, which, although unknown to him at the time, coincides significantly with the footprint of the demon Amduscias, illustrated in the 1863 edition of Collin de Plancy's *Dictionnaire infernal*.

The consistency of UFO sightings over

Clapham Wood continued during 1978 and 1979, one being reported by a man standing on nearby Highdown Hill, which is higher than Clapham and overlooks the woods. The witness says he saw a large orange ball about twice the size of an aircraft, which manoeuvred above the woods for some 20 minutes before disappearing. And several independent witnesses from different vantage points reported seeing a huge light in the sky above Clapham Wood one summer's night in 1979. It descended vertically into the woods and glowed among the trees.

Could it be explained away as mere coincidence? It seems unlikely with so many people coming forward with similar stories of sightings all made at the same time.

The spate of strange reports that year concluded with the disappearance of the Reverend Neil Snelling, vicar of Clapham church. One fine morning after shopping at Worthing he decided to walk back to his Steyning home through Clapham Wood. Almost certainly he would have taken the 'Chestnuts' route. He has not been heard of since, and an exhaustive search of the area revealed nothing.

What happened to him? Why did the dogs

Right: a photograph taken by Paul Glover. He saw nothing at the time, although he felt intense cold – but when the photograph was developed, it showed a goat's head, age-old symbol of satanism

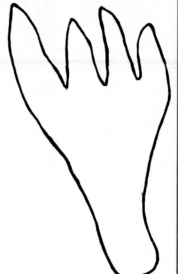

disappear so completely within only a few yards of their unsuspecting owners? How can solid bodies vanish into thin air without leaving a trace? Is there a deadly chemical in the soil, or some unknown force that disrupts the molecular structure of organic creatures? Did a meteorite – or some unknown object from space – once fall in the area, and if so, is it giving off harmful rays or acting as a beacon for UFOs?

So many independent reports cannot be ignored, but real proof of the phenomena is not easy to come by. It was in the hope of obtaining some form of proof that Paul Glover armed himself with a camera and, accompanied by Dave Stringer and another friend, made for Clapham Wood.

It was a dark, clear evening, but there was no UFO activity. Eventually they decided to make their way homewards via the Chestnuts route, and it was as they were walking through this area that all three of them, simultaneously, had a feeling of intense cold. They hurried on, and the feeling ceased. So they walked back over the same area – three times in fact – and each time experienced this sudden and unnatural drop in temperature.

Glover decided to point the camera at what he thought was the source of this strange condition, seeing nothing, but firing the shutter purely on speculation.

When the photograph was developed, however, it showed an uncanny white mass revealing the unmistakable image of a goat's head, the age-old symbol of satanic rites. Was this confirmation of the past – or present – activities of a black coven? Or was it quite separate, adding yet another phenomenon to the enigma of Clapham Wood?

Satan in the snow

One cold February morning in 1855 a strange trail of footprints was found in the thick snow that covered South Devon. No one could tell what had caused them and, as GRAHAM FULLER and IAN KNIGHT explain, the villagers began to fear that they were the marks of the Devil himself

THE WEATHER in the winter of 1855 was very much on the minds of the Victorian public. In the Crimea a British army was slowly dying of exposure, its death throes meticulously chronicled in *The Times* and the illustrated weeklies. At home the Thames was frozen at Kingston and the adventurous were to be seen skating on the Serpentine. In the west of England isolated villages were cut off by flurries of snow; local bakers were unable to bring supplies to the stranded community of Lustleigh in Devon, and in Torquay hundreds were out of work due to the icy conditions. In February the ice on the River Exe was so thick at one point that gas was laid on from the street and revellers cooked a substantial meal; further west the River Teign froze in several places and the sea wall at Teignmouth collapsed, taking with it a section of the railway. Unwary travellers caught out overnight perished in the freezing temperatures.

The night of Thursday, 8 February must have seemed like any other to the inhabitants of the towns and villages along the Exe estuary. There was a heavy fall of snow in the early part of the night, followed by rain, a bitter wind and, in the morning, frost. Yet, accustomed though they were to the peculiarities of nature at her worst, the morning of the 9th gave them something of a surprise. As *The Times* reported on 16 February:

> Considerable sensation has been evoked in the towns of Topsham, Lympstone, Exmouth, Teignmouth, and Dawlish, in the south of Devon, in consequence of the discovery of a vast number of foot-tracks of a most strange and mysterious description. The superstitious go so far as to believe that they are the marks of Satan himself; and that great excitement has been produced among all classes may be judged from the fact that the subject has been descanted on from the pulpit.

It appears that on Thursday night last there was a very heavy fall of snow

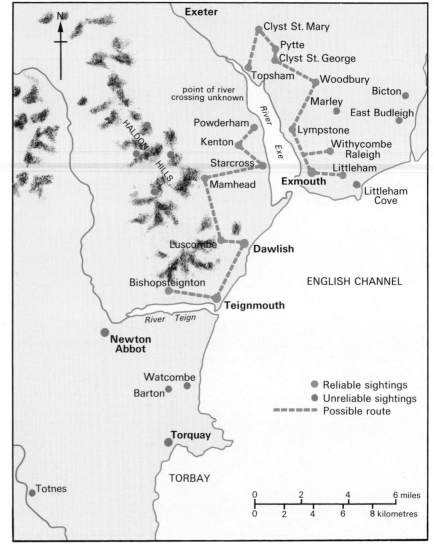

Below: the Thames frozen at Richmond in 1855. That winter was exceptionally severe all over England: villages were cut off, food supplies were restricted, and many people died of the cold

in the neighbourhood of Exeter and the south of Devon. On the following morning, the inhabitants of the above towns were surprised at discovering the tracks of some strange and mysterious animal, endowed with the power of ubiquity, as the footprints were to be seen in all kinds of inaccessible places – on the tops of houses and narrow walls, in gardens and courtyards enclosed by high walls and palings, as well as in open fields. There was hardly a garden in Lympstone where the footprints were not observed.

The track appeared more like that of a biped than a quadruped, and the steps were generally eight inches [20 centimetres] in advance of each other. The impressions of the feet closely resembled that of a donkey's shoe, and measured from an inch and a half [4 centimetres] to (in some instances) two and a half inches [6 centimetres] across. Here and there it appeared as if cloven, but in the generality of the steps the shoe was continuous, and, from the snow in the centre remaining entire, merely showing the outer crest of the

Left: reported sightings of the mysterious footprints in South Devon in February 1855, and the possible route taken (assuming that all the prints were made by the same entity). The trail stops at Bishopsteignton to the west of the River Exe and at Littleham to the east. The point at which the river was crossed is unknown, but it could have been at Topsham where the Exe is only a few hundred yards wide

foot, it must have been convex. [Probably an error – this description and all other accounts indicate that the foot must have been concave.]

The creature seems to have approached the doors of several houses and then to have retreated, but no-one has been able to discover the standing or resting point of the mysterious visitor . . .

At present it remains a mystery, and many superstitious people in the above towns are actually afraid to go outside their doors after night.

Certainly, the appearance of the unidentified footprints overnight, covering such a large area, caused something of a stir. At Dawlish, where the tracks went right through the village, the local hunt set out, accompanied by villagers with guns and clubs, to follow the tracks, 'till at last, in a wood, the hounds came back baying and terrified'. Rumour had

it that many of the marks clearly indicated that the foot that made them was cloven; other reports said it had claws. For the majority of the country-folk, this evidence led to one inescapable conclusion: 'The sages of Lympstone pronounced the *vestigia utiorsum* to be decidedly Satanic: and an Exmouth old woman has taken the occasion to remind us that Satan was to be unchained for a thousand years.' The effect, according to 'G.M.M.', a correspondent to the *Illustrated London News*, was that

labourers, their wives and children, and old crones, and trembling old men [dreaded] to stir out after sunset, or to go out half a mile into lanes or byways, on a call or message, under the conviction that this was the Devil's walk, and none other, and that it was wicked to trifle with such a manifest proof of the Great Enemy's immediate presence . . .

Following the footprints

Fortunately several observers on the spot were sufficiently scientific in their approach to leave detailed records of the phenomenon. Writing from Newport House, Countess Wear, in the heart of the affected area, a Mr D'Urban, grandson of the man who gave his name to Durban in South Africa, reported what he had seen:

The marks . . . to all appearance were the perfect impression of a donkey's hoof – the length 4 inches by $2\frac{3}{4}$ inches [10 centimetres by 7 centimetres]; but, instead of progressing as that animal would have done (or indeed as any other would have done), feet right and left, it appeared that foot had followed foot, in a *single line*; the distance from each tread being eight inches [20 centimetres], or rather more . . . This mysterious visitor generally only passed *once* down or across each garden or courtyard, and did so in nearly all the houses in many parts of several towns . . . also in the farms scattered about; this regular track passing in some instances over the roofs of houses, and hayricks, and very high walls . . . without displacing the snow on either side or altering the distance between the feet, and passing on as if the wall had not been any impediment.

Two reverend gentlemen, G. M. Musgrave of Exmouth (the 'G.M.M.' of the *Illustrated London News* columns) and H. T. Ellacombe of Clyst St George, spent some time and energy both following the footprints and corresponding with neighbours on the subject. Their descriptions of the track, which climbed over roofs, under bushes 8 inches (20 centimetres) from the ground, through a 6-inch (15-centimetre) drainpipe, and finally stopped dead in the middle of a field outside Exmouth, need not be doubted. 'My dog barked that night, and so did the dogs of my neighbour where the marks were seen,'

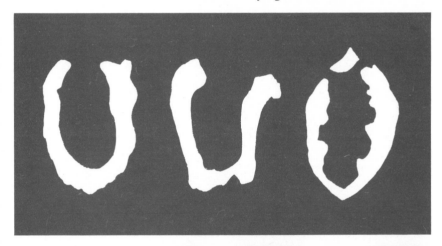

Above: these drawings of the footprints were made by the Reverend G.M. Musgrave and published in the *Illustrated London News* with an accompanying letter. In an attempt to allay the fears of his parishioners, Musgrave suggested that the prints could be those of a kangaroo that was reported to have escaped from a nearby private zoo

Right: a hoofed Devil from a 15th-century stained glass window by Hans Acker. To the superstitious among the inhabitants of South Devon there was no doubt that the footprints in the snow were the marks of Satan himself

commented Ellacombe, significantly.

Inevitably, the reports encouraged a welter of correspondence from people convinced that they held the key to the mystery. It was variously suggested that the visitor was an otter, a crane, a swan, an escaped kangaroo, even a rat jumping with all four feet together, and that the strange shape of the prints was due to atmospheric conditions. Richard Owen, a leading naturalist of the day, studied some drawings made by Ellacombe and pronounced the marks to be the tracks of a badger. Others, mindful that the trail passed over rooftops and appeared on high window-sills, believed a bird was responsible – the hoof-shaped impression caused by ice on its toes. Though more feasible than most, since large flocks of birds were known to have been sheltering in the estuary, this explanation still failed to convince everyone. D'Urban had recently

> passed a five months' winter in the backwoods of Canada, and has had much experience in tracking wild animals and birds upon the snow, and can safely say, he has never seen a more clearly-defined track, or one that appeared to be less altered by the atmosphere than the one in question . . . No known animal could have traversed this extent of country in one night, besides having to cross an estuary of the sea two miles [3 kilometres] broad. Neither does any known animal walk in a *line* of single footsteps, not even man . . . no bird's foot leaves the impression of a hoof.

'A superstitious folly'

So, is it possible, after 125 years, to discover just what did visit South Devon that winter's night in 1855, causing such 'a superstitious folly'? By carefully sifting contemporary accounts, it is, at least, possible to obtain a better picture of the nature of the mystery. First, though D'Urban later became a respected antiquary, noted for his careful reporting, he was only 19 in 1855, and his writings may have been swayed by over-enthusiasm and hearsay. There is no evidence, certainly, to support his claim that the trail started as far west as Totnes, and only a little to verify its presence at Torquay; most independent accounts suggest that it started west of Teignmouth, passed through Dawlish, travelled northwards on the west side of the Exe estuary and then southwards on the east side, ending outside Exmouth – a much shorter distance than has sometimes been claimed. Only at its mouth is the Exe 2 miles (3 kilometres) wide, and the reports indicate that the mysterious visitor may have walked across the frozen river as far up as Topsham, where it narrows to a few hundred yards. The probability that it passed on the north side of the Teign estuary and on either side of the Exe – as if the creature were trying to avoid crossing water – discredits the rather

Left: Sir Richard Owen, a leading naturalist of the time. In a letter to the *Illustrated London News* of 3 March 1855 he expressed his considered opinion that the footprints were those of a badger (below). The badger is, he remarked, a nocturnal creature that 'comes abroad occasionally in the late winter, when hard-pressed by cold and hunger'. With such footprints, he said, 'those of the fore and hind-foot are commonly more or less blended together, producing the appearance of a line of single footsteps'

Above: the Reverend H.T. Ellacombe, of Clyst St George. He said that some of the prints looked as if they had been made with a branding iron or by carving shapes into the snow with a knife

outlandish 'sea monster theory' that was favoured by some.

Miss Theo Brown, a lecturer at Exeter University and Recorder of Folklore for the Devonshire Association, has studied the case and collected oral traditions relating to it, and believes that some of the marks can be eliminated. At Topsham the tracks were not seen until St Valentine's Day, several days after their appearance elsewhere, suggesting that not all the prints appeared simultaneously, as some described. There are slight differences, too, between the known drawings of the tracks – so maybe they did not share a common origin. Some so clearly resembled a donkey's shoe that they may have been just that, mistaken for something more mysterious in the uproar. Others looked, said Ellacombe, 'as if the snow had been branded with a hot iron or the form of such a shoe had been cut out with a knife to the ground', and may have been the work of practical jokers. Certain of the affected parishes were at the time dallying with Puseyism, a neo-Catholic revival suspected of being rather too Roman, and the fact that the prints went up to the church door in several of these parishes hints at a human agency seeking to point the finger; certainly one local newspaper referred to a belief that the visitation was 'a warning to the Puseyites'.

Nevertheless, it is not possible to explain away the heart of the mystery. There were 'some thousands of these marks . . . extending over many miles of either side of the Exe and Clyst': even if one discounts a number for the reasons mentioned, the vast majority occurred overnight, and were sufficiently strange to throw the locals – who, like all country-folk, would have known a badger track from that of a rat or a swan – into a state of panic. The so-called 'Great Devon Mystery' remains exactly that.

It is not, however, the only case of mysterious prints in the snow. The *Western Times* reported that 'a similar occurrence

Above: Edward Pusey, a leader of the 19th-century neo-Catholic revival. Some critics of Puseyism saw the footprints as a sign that followers of the movement were possessed by the Devil

took place here about five years ago' (that is, in about 1850). Subsequent observers have been quick to point out that in May 1840, while on an exploratory trip to the Antarctic, Captain Sir James Clark Ross stopped off at the uninhabited, largely frozen Kerguelen Island and found in the snow unidentifiable 'traces . . . of the singular footprints of a pony, or ass, being 3 inches [7.5 centimetres] in length and $2\frac{1}{2}$ [6 centimetres] in breadth, having a small deeper depression in either side, and shaped like a horseshoe'.

In Scotland, also in 1840, similar tracks were reported 'among the mountains where Glenorchy, Glenlyon and Glenochay are contiguous'. One correspondent, in the wake of the Devon incident, reported that on Piashowa-gora ('sand hill'), a small elevation on the border of Galicia, such marks were to be seen in the snow every year, 'and are attributed by the local inhabitants to supernatural influences'. Footprints left by an apparently one-legged, cloven-footed beast in parts of Inverness at the same time as the 'Devil's hoofmarks' appeared in Devon excited some local speculation but were later explained away by a passing naturalist as the tracks of a hare or polecat. In 1945 science-fiction writer Eric Frank Russell, while serving with the Allied army during the Ardennes campaign, reported seeing similar impressions in the snow. The local people were at a loss to explain them; unfortunately the scarcity of film prevented Russell from making a permanent record.

The question remains. Just what is it that can cover large areas of snowbound countryside in a short space of time, undeterred by obstacles, running in a fast, mincing step and leaving a hoof-shaped footprint?

About 15 years before the mysterious markings were seen in Devon, the English explorer Sir James Clark Ross (above) had discovered strange single-track prints in the snow at Kerguelen Island (right), which lies near the Antarctic Circle. Called the 'island of desolation', Kerguelen was then uninhabited; seals and seabirds were the only wildlife to be found there. Yet Ross reported the prints he saw as being those of 'a pony or ass . . . and shaped like a horseshoe'

Index